D0303925

Understanding Children's Experiences
of Parental Bereavement

Understanding Children's Experiences of Parental Bereavement

John Holland

Jessica Kingsley Publishers
London and Philadelphia

All rights reserved. No paragraph of this publication may be reproduced, copied or transmitted save with written permission of the Copyright Act 1956 (as amended), or under the terms of any licence permitting limited copying issued by the Copyright Licensing Agency, 33–34 Alfred Place, London WC1E 7DP. Any person who does any unauthorised act in relation to this publication may be liable to prosecution and civil claims for damages.

The right of John Holland to be identified as author of this work has been asserted by him in accordance with the Copyright, Designs and Patents Act 1988.

First published in the United Kingdom in 2001 by
Jessica Kingsley Publishers Ltd,
116 Pentonville Road, London
N1 9JB, England
and
325 Chestnut Street,
Philadelphia, PA 19106, USA.

www.jkp.com

© Copyright 2001 John Holland

Library of Congress Cataloging in Publication Data
A CIP catalog record for this book is available from the Library of Congress

British Library Cataloguing in Publication Data
A CIP catalogue record for this book is available from the British Library

ISBN 1 84310 016 9

Printed and Bound in Great Britain by
Athenaeum Press, Gateshead, Tyne and Wear

Contents

Tables

Acknowledgements

Thanks to Sue May for her support and encouragement, and the Iceberg volunteers for sharing their stories.

Introduction

This book gives an insight into the world of children who have experienced the death of a parent. It is based on the findings of Iceberg, a doctoral project carried out at the University of York, in which adults who had been bereaved of a parent when they were of school age or under agreed to share their experiences. I wrote the book after a decade of research within the area of loss and bereavement in schools, initially as an infant class teacher, later as a peripatetic special needs teacher, and subsequently as an educational psychologist, all within the Humberside area. My concern was that children's experience of bereavement could be fundamentally quite different from the adult experience. The death of a parent may have far-reaching implications for children, even into adulthood. The voices of bereaved children are not always heard and youngsters may be disempowered, for example by being forbidden to attend their parent's funeral. Iceberg investigated the role of the adult world in helping or hindering these children, and sought their views on how things could have been improved. Many of the volunteers taking part in Iceberg felt that the adult world was of little help to them at the time of their parents' deaths, and that they had been let down by the adult world. They often felt powerless after the death of a parent and lacked the means to gain information, frequently feeling that they faced a wall of silence.

The book will be of interest and use to any professionals who come into contact with bereaved children, particularly in the context of schools. Parents and other adults may also find that the book provides an insight from those who have gone through the experience of a parent dying. 'Loss' covers many of life's experiences, and although the focus of the book is on bereavement, a loss through death, much is also relevant in terms of other losses encountered by youngsters. The impact of these other losses may well mirror many of the experiences of bereaved children:

- Parental separation: the break-up of a child's family can also lead to significant losses.

- Children being 'looked after': there are increasingly more children who are in the 'looked after' situation and have experienced the loss of their birth family.

- Special educational needs: both parents and children may have a loss response as they become increasingly aware of the special needs. Parents may have to change their expectations of their children, and children may perceive that they differ from their peers.

- Children encounter various transitions throughout their school life, such as the move from primary to secondary school, perhaps from a small primary school to a larger comprehensive school on split sites with several subject teachers. These transitions also involve elements of loss and change.

For very young children there may be no difference for them between the loss of a carer by death or by absence. A significant person has left the life of the young child either permanently or temporarily, and they may not distinguish the difference. This could equally be the case in the event of a loss of a parent by relationship separation. Iceberg found that the experiences of death for adults are significantly different from the youngest children. There are many other children in a grey area, not experiencing death in the same way as adults, but having a greater appreciation of the difference between absence and death, than did their younger peers. This group of youngsters was a focus for Iceberg, and there were both similarities and significant differences in the reactions of these children when compared with adults.

Guide to the book

This brief section gives a guide to the book. Chapter 1 outlines the background to the projects that preceded Iceberg. These initial studies took place mainly in the eastern region of England, and looked at the experiences and perceptions of teachers in relation to children who were bereaved of a parent when they were at school. In contrast the Iceberg project focused on the experiences and stories of children who had been through the experience of a parent dying.

In Chapter 2 the issues of loss and change are discussed as life experiences, and death is also put in an historical context. Our experience of and contact with death are significantly different in many ways from the experiences of our ancestors. The contemporary experience of death includes effects such as the media, and the impact this can have on our perceptions of death. The differences between death as a personal loss and also in a public sense are contrasted here; we now seem to experience much more vicarious grieving through the media, with those with whom we do not have a personal relationship. The importance of the post death rituals is also mentioned.

Chapter 3 examines some of the traditional theoretical models in the area of loss, including the 'stage' and 'task' models of grieving, as well as the idea of 'continuing bonds', that we continue the relationship with the deceased and do not 'detach' from them. Models are explanations, attempts to explain the world to gain a better understanding and to focus on the key main elements, although they do have the potential danger of oversimplification and over-generalisation. This chapter is a backdrop against which the results of Iceberg are later discussed, as it was found that the more traditional models did not always translate to the actual experiences of the Iceberg volunteers, who were all children at the time of the bereavement.

Chapter 4 looks at the importance of schema and language, both ways through which we gain a cognitive understanding of death. Children will use language, through both their thoughts and communications with others, to help them to gain this greater understanding of death. There could be problems of understanding if children's death schema is obtained from the media, rather than from personal experience, which would have been how this knowledge was acquired in the not so distant past. Language may also confuse children, such as the use of euphemisms for death, like 'popped his clogs', and the need to avoid the use of complex medical terms; great care needs to be given with explanations. Children may think that a person has literally been 'lost' or become confused by medical terminology, or even by explanations such as a 'heart attack'. How can a heart be attacked? The language used to explain things needs to reflect the cognitive level and also the life experience of the youngster.

Chapters 5 to 7 provide a backdrop to the results of the Iceberg research which is described in the later chapters. This backdrop generally relates to the adult based perceptions rather than the stories of bereaved children. Chapter 5 reviews childhood bereavement in general, including its frequency and the effects previously noticed by adults in children who have experienced the death of a parent.

Chapter 6 discusses some of the issues surrounding how bereaved children could be supported by their school and this is returned to in later chapters.

Chapter 7 reviews the background to children's understanding of death, and this is also returned to as a subject in later chapters.

Chapter 8 provides the background to the Iceberg research itself, explaining how it took a different approach from many other studies, by using the experiences of bereaved children themselves. Adults who were bereaved of a parent when they were children were asked to reflect on their childhood experiences and to share these experiences with the author. The method used for the study, how the volunteers were obtained, and some ethical and methodological issues are also discussed. These include issues of memory and a brief discussion of the analysis stage.

Chapter 9 introduces the results of the Iceberg project. These are shown in themes, which are not necessarily related to the order of the questions in the interview schedule.

Chapter 10 focuses on events at the time of the death of the parent. These include the initial reactions of the Iceberg volunteers to the news of the death of their parent and also their initial understanding of the events at the time. The pattern of the volunteers' initial reactions was very similar to the adult models of grieving, apart from the lack of understanding as to what was happening at the time.

Chapter 11 revolves around the theme of two common rituals after many deaths, visiting the body of the parent at the chapel of rest and attending the funeral.

The theme of Chapter 12 is the return to school after the death, and how the school responded as well as how the response could have been improved.

Chapter 13 considers the theme of isolation and how isolated many Iceberg volunteers felt during the first year after the death. Neither teachers nor other adults were easy to approach to discuss the death. Most of the volunteers discussed the death with nobody or with just one person.

Chapter 14 considers the Iceberg volunteers' experiences over the following periods: one month, six months, one year and two years after the death.

Chapter 15 discusses the theme of the medium and long-term effects of the death, and Chapter 16 looks at the age when the Iceberg volunteers first grasped the idea of death.

In Chapter 17 the various types of losses reported by the Iceberg volunteers are discussed. These relate to issues of attachment, bereavement or mourning the death of an individual, collateral loss flowing from the death, such as moving house or school. The final two are delayed loss, realised only later in life, and expected loss, that which is predictable, but has not yet occurred, and flowing from the death.

Chapter 18 relates how the experience of death is different for children compared to the adult experience, for example in terms of power, control and information.

Chapter 19 draws together and examines the answers from the formal research questions raised, and their implications.

Finally the book concludes with appendices showing the question sheets used in the research.

Chapter 1

The Humberside studies and Iceberg

The projects

My initial research into the field of loss and bereavement in schools was in the Humberside area of England, and investigated how primary schools responded to parental death and childhood bereavement (Holland 1993). This was shortly followed by a similar study in Humberside secondary schools, which was carried out jointly with Corinne Ludford (Holland and Ludford 1995). These studies established that there was a 'training gap', in that schools recognised that bereavement was an important area, but were sometimes unsure as to how they could best help their pupils. The identification of this training gap led to some joint training of teachers which was carried out by the Hull based Dove House Hospice and professionals from the former Humberside County Council. This ultimately led to a 'loss awareness' training package for teachers, named 'Lost for Words', being developed by Kingston upon Hull Learning Services.

I also carried out a cross-cultural study with Louise Rowling, comparing how Australian and English schools responded to issues of loss, bereavement and suicide (Rowling and Holland 2000). During a period in Newcastle upon Tyne, I carried out a study with secondary schools in the north-east of England, comparing how the schools responded to parental death and parental separation (Holland 2000).

These projects were all carried out with teachers and schools, and both primary and secondary schools rated the area of bereavement relatively highly. There were some teachers who were very confident in dealing with loss and death, although schools generally considered that they needed more training to increase their levels of skill. Schools tended to have a reactive approach to bereavement, dealing with each death on an ad-hoc basis, rather than having a systematic planned response. Teachers often contended that, as bereavement is an individual experience, all deaths needed an individual response. Bereavements are of course all individual, but it is also possible to have general policies and systems in place and prepared at a time of calm, rather than waiting until a death has occurred when there may be more of a crisis.

There seemed to be a connection between the lack of policies and systems, the ad-hoc approach, and the lack of expertise in schools. School policies and procedures are potentially very important vehicles in helping to effect change, but without teachers feeling comfortable and skilled in the area of bereavement and loss, then it is unlikely that change will take place in schools. Local authorities can also foster change – for example, as mentioned above, the training package for teachers entitled 'Lost for Words', launched in October 2000 with the intention of raising teachers' levels of awareness about loss and bereavement.

Schools in the research often reported that bereaved youngsters presented with problems in behaviour and learning. These reports seemed to make sense in terms of the emotional roller-coasters which individuals often feel that they are riding after a significant loss. Emotions such as anger, a frequent response to a loss, could potentially result in behaviour difficulties at school, with youngsters having short fuses and displaying verbal or aggressive outbursts. While these behaviours are not condoned, the source of the youngster's anger could be misinterpreted or the context not fully understood. This could particularly be the case if the behaviour occurs some time after the loss event. The youngster may be perceived by staff as having recovered from their loss, and the behaviour perhaps not seen as a contextual issue. In a similar way, depression and sadness after a loss could lead to apathy, a lack of focus and concentration with a subsequent decline in academic attainments. The loss event again may not be connected with the behaviour displayed. Children may also move both classes and schools and their new teachers may not be aware of the loss.

In summary, the schools in the various studies I had carried out rated the area of child bereavement relatively highly, and recognised that they had training needs. Schools were also aware of both behaviour and learning difficulties after a death. The previous research had a school and teacher based focus and this was only part of the total, the missing link being the experiences of the bereaved youngsters themselves. The adults both at school and at home may not share the same perceptions as the bereaved children with whom they interacted. It seemed important to investigate the experience of parental death from the point of view of the youngster, and this led directly to Iceberg, the doctoral research project, carried out through the University of York.

Iceberg

Iceberg was named to represent the potentially large amount of unrecognised grief and other effects that youngsters may experience after the death of a parent. I began the project in 1995 at the University of York, completing it in 2000, having had a year at the University of Newcastle to train as an educational psychologist. Iceberg was intended to gain a reflective insight into the experiences and perceptions of bereaved young people. Nearly 100 volunteers took part in the project, which was carried out by interview and questionnaire; 70 of the Iceberg volunteers were adults who had been bereaved of a parent when they were at school and these formed the core group.

Researching the area of death is fraught with difficulties and needs a sensitive approach. There are ethical issues in carrying out research with bereaved children as well as with recently bereaved adults. Not only could this be an unwanted intrusion, but also it has the potential of causing further distress. Because of these ethical issues, I included only adults in Iceberg, and only those bereaved at least five years before their interview. The advantage was that these volunteers were able to respond after at least five years' reflection upon their experiences. Although I was unable to offer counselling, I was able to guide those with grieving difficulties to where they could seek further support.

Chapter 2

Change and losses in the cultural context

Change

Change varies, from the smallest, such as shifting our gaze, to a major change such as emigrating to another country. We seem to have the capacity to cope with some degree of change, but may become overloaded and suffer a negative psychological impact or loss reaction if this capacity is exceeded. Our inability to control the change event may affect our loss response, as may our life experiences and our previously learnt coping strategies. Being out of control of events could well add to stress and to the loss reaction, and this may be an issue with children. Loss in life results from any change that impacts so greatly as to overwhelm us and become problematic. Loss is an individual experience and the impact it has will depend on our personality and previous experiences.

Separation and loss

Grief is an emotional response to a loss, bereavement being the state of actually losing something, a term conventionally used in loss by death, with mourning the outward expression of our internal experience of grief (Goldman 1994). Death and trauma may or may not occur together, individuals may survive a traumatic experience, such as being under fire in a war-zone or being involved in a horrific accident. It could be argued that any death brings with it an element of trauma for the survivors, and that stress and crisis are always present in any bereavement, being physiological and psychological reactions to a loss event (Cannon 1929). Where trauma is defined as witnessing a horrific event, a specialist intervention such as critical incident stress debriefing may be needed. Where bereavement after a death is problematic, a counselling response may be appropriate, although most bereaved are unlikely to need specialist intervention.

We may mourn for other losses or changes in our life, such as the temporary parting from a loved one. Evidence of a loss reaction in children's responses when separated from their mother while she was in hospital for the birth of another child has been found (Field and Reite 1984). The reactions reported included agitated behaviour, often followed by depression and increased illness, hinting at changes in the child's immune system and resistance to infections. Similar effects have been found when children moved house, or when they passed through a transition such has starting a new school (Fried 1962). Experiences of these small losses may be important in the acquisition of loss coping strategies. If we are able to cope with small losses, then our ability to cope with the larger losses in life could be greater. There is no absolute hierarchy of loss, as each one will depend on individual perception, bonding and attachment to that which has been lost.

The concept of attachment seems plausible as a survival technique and mechanism to maintain us within social groups and the reaction to loss may have evolutionary origins in relation to social cohesion. The human infant is vulnerable and dependent, and may be hard-wired with the need to stay with the group.

Death in a cultural setting

Our experience of and reaction to death are set in the context of time and place. Grief seems to be a universal human characteristic, although its display in a particular form is culturally determined (Archer 1999). Burial rituals, evidenced by graves, can be traced back over 500,000 years. In more recent times, the pyramids in Egypt were intrinsically linked with the notion of the afterlife, suggesting the importance of death rituals for that culture. The focus of these rites, as later with the Vikings, was the passing of the deceased to a new state, rather than with the remaining mourners. A visitor to the Great Pyramids and Sphinx in Giza cannot fail to find these structures impressive, an indication of the status they held within the culture.

Our general contemporary view of death does contrast with the Egyptian or Viking view and is a reflection of the status which death holds within our society. It has been suggested that there was a gradual shift in our attitudes toward death from the Middle Ages to current times (Ariès 1983). During the Middle Ages, death seemed to be accepted stoically with resignation: life expectancy was just 33 years. Death gradually became more of an event for the individual, later to be feared, with the notion of hell and divine retribution. By the nineteenth century death was seen as a reintegration into the next life. The control of death seems to have shifted from the individual to the family and then to the professionals. Until the early part of the twentieth century, children were intimately involved with death, which usually happened within the family setting. The creation of childhood, a relatively modern concept, that contrasts to being a young family member may have accelerated this process.

The antecedents to bereavement, including the specific circumstances of the individual and the social setting, are likely part determinants of grieving (Parkes 1986). Queen Victoria is an example, being so dependent on Prince Albert that her grieving seemed lengthy, abnormal and without resolution.

The contemporary status of death in western culture, often seen as a taboo subject, contrasts with many cultures across the world having a more fatalistic approach, with death seeming to present far less of a terror to the individual. In some ways, our approach to death is really quite primitive; we seem to consider quite irrationally that death can be avoided (Illich 1977). Generally we do not have the open public grieving which is tolerated and even expected at funerals in some cultures around the world. The sight of open grieving may be quite alien and difficult to understand, but in reality such expressions of feelings may be both positive and therapeutic for those in mourning. Maoris believe that if you do not let feelings out, then there is no physically or emotional healing. Maori children have an important involvement in this process.

Public and personal experiences of death

Although death is not usually encountered frequently in our personal life, this is not the case in the media. News and communications travels apace today, through satellites, television and the Internet. Death is often shown as a fearful and traumatic event, without such it would probably not be of media interest. In psychological terms, we perhaps have a 'death schema' formed from the evidence around us, especially in the media. Major disasters such as the crash of Pan Am Flight 103 on Lockerbie or the Hillsborough football stadium disaster do attract much public and media attention. The survivors and bereaved of these very public tragedies generally gain support from the caring professions and the event is very much in the public arena. Traumatic or violent fatalities, such as suicides or murder, are also likely to be more in the public arena, especially when they involve celebrities, such as Diana, Princess of Wales, and the television presenter Jill Dando. These deaths do seem to invoke a public grief reaction, although this is not a bereavement reaction in the sense that there is no personal bond or personal loss with those who experience the death only vicariously through the media. These events, which are atypical deaths, may well reinforce a general perception of death as a violent, not a peaceful, ending to life, which may be quite misleading. We may now subconsciously perceive of death as the act of 'being killed', rather than having an image of dying relatively peacefully of old age (Kubler-Ross 1982). The focus of the book is not on these public deaths. Death without trauma or celebrity involvement rarely makes headline news, although it will likely have far-reaching effects for the bereaved. Most deaths receive no public recognition other than the funeral and a mention in the local obituary column. This is a 'quieter' problem, though it has potential major consequences for the bereaved, especially for children where a parent has died. Adult children too will not be untouched by the death of their parent.

It seems strange that our general culture appears not to cope well with death, especially as it is the one and only inevitable event to overtake us all. Death does seem to have been sanitised and taken out of the context of the family, partly through public health legislation. The family has slowly but surely ceded ground in the area of death to the professionals. Today, we tend to rely on various professionals, such as undertakers and doctors, at times of death, and for other support agencies, such as counsellors, to help us through our grief. We expect professionals to 'undertake' matters in the area of death on our behalf, in sharp contrast to some other cultures and our own past history. In the past children would not have needed death education, since death was so much more a part of life. There could still today be a distinction between urban and rural children, as the latter will probably have more of an opportunity to see nature in the raw (Leaman 1995). As our exposure to death has declined so perhaps our difficulties with the area have increased. If parents are uncomfortable with the subject of death, then it is not surprising that their children have the same difficulty. This is a generalisation, as some communities and individuals within our culture do seem to cope better at times of death.

Those who have been bereaved will often receive much support at the time of the death, but this may decline in the medium or long term. They may later be actively avoided, perhaps because of embarrassment or the perceived fear of the reaction of the bereft. Well-meaning individuals may not know what to say or how to approach the subject of the death. Families may now be separated in distance from an extended family support system, and religion may not play the same role in providing support. Without religious belief, death may perhaps be perceived as a final act and the end of existence for that individual. This would make the perceived loss of the bereaved far greater than in the past, where the deceased was thought of as going on to 'better things'. There is less surprising evidence suggesting that the support of friends and acquaintances is much valued by the bereaved (Rosenblatt 1988). This does make the assumption that these friends can offer appropriate support, but hints that teachers and other adults could potentially fulfil this role for children. It seems plausible to suggest that how well children cope with the area of death and bereavement in their adult life is partly a function of their childhood experiences, and how the adults around them at that time dealt with these losses.

The importance of rituals

Rites and rituals seem to be important in the period of transition for the bereaved, who is 'between states' in the social sense (Turner 1969). There needs to be a period of adjustment to the change, straight after the death, as the world of the individual could have greatly changed. Today, we tend to be less involved in rituals that provide an element of continuity, as well as certainty to the bereavement process, to past generations. Local women once played a role in the laying out of bodies in English rural areas. Knowledge was passed down the generations from mother to daughter, until the Midwifery Act of 1902 severed this link, excluding many of the women from involvement in these processes (Chamberlain and Richardson 1983). Not only do we generally encounter death on a less frequent basis, but also the encounter may not be on the personal level of being actively involved in the rites and rituals. Victorian children were as used to going to funerals as they were to weddings and they took an active part in the death rituals, such as helping to lay out the body (Musty 1990). Children may lack this opportunity, and the knowledge of what is happening after a death; many may not have seen a corpse, nor viewed the body of a relation. Bereaved relatives are generally helped in their grief by having access to the body of the deceased after a hospital death (Wright 1989). Viewing the body would likely help the relations to come to terms with the death and also help to minimise denial. The lack of information around death may present ideal conditions for the growth of children's fantasies and myths around the subject, which may well far outstrip the reality of what is happening.

The importance of the funeral is that it strengthens social bonds through obliging large numbers of people to share and to show their emotions after a death, and it is one of the few remaining rituals relating to death (Barnsley 1995). The funeral is an important rite and a stage in the bereaved beginning to start their adjustment to the new circumstances of their life (Marshall 1993). Mothers may perhaps discourage their children from attending the rites after the death, apparently to protect them (Marris 1958). By not allowing a child to attend the funeral of their parent, there is the danger that an environment of denial may be created, which could inhibit children's grieving (Goldman 1994).

Other former rituals after a death included the drawing of curtains in the house, the shuttering of the house windows, the laying out the body at home, and black being worn for a prescribed period of time. It was the women rather than the men who were expected to wear mourning clothes (Taylor 1983). These prescribed conventions were both clear and unambiguous, providing a large amount of certainty to all and clarity as to actions. The Victorian age of death rites ended with the First World War: perhaps the number of people who were killed during those relatively few years was so overwhelming that it led to the decline in the former practices (Gorer 1965). Today there seems to be little guidance as to how to behave after a death occurs. The bereaved is likely to be in emotional shock during the time immediately after the death, and may be therefore lacking in rational judgement. The decline in these rites may relate to an increase in psychological problems for the bereaved (Gorer 1965). Rites, such as having contact with the body of the deceased, especially when it is retained in the home before the burial or the cremation, would arguably help to emphasise the reality of the death to the bereaved.

Today, we generally seem more uncertain about how to behave after a death. In addition, there is a reduced frequency of encountering death, as infant mortality and life expectancy at birth have tended to decrease and increase respectively over time. Infant mortality has been reduced from 142 per thousand live births in 1900 to just 5.7 per thousand in 1998 (Cental Statistical Office (CSO) 1989; Office for National Statistics 1999). The average life expectancy of life for males at birth in 1906 was 48 years; this had increased to 75.1 by 1999.

Chapter 3

The 'traditional' models of loss

Introduction to models of loss

The importance of models is that they are attempts to provide explanations. Models in the social sciences are problematic, in that they are dealing with human behaviour. To experiment with behaviour in a laboratory, such as with other sciences, leads to the removal of the general context, and may not adequately reflect real life. Models are helpful in terms of providing guidance and, with death, providing a framework on which to hang the experience of bereavement. They offer some explanation as to what is happening in a loss situation, although perhaps it is important to use them as rough guides rather than to be too dogmatic. Our cultural focus has tended to be on disengaging from the deceased, with notions such as the 'resolution of grief' and 'investing emotional energy elsewhere' tending to predominate. The disengagement model of grief could be regarded as a phenomenon of the twentieth century (Silverman and Klass 1996). It could be argued that Freud founded this type of grief work, relating to the reinvestment of mental energy away from the dead person (Freud 1917). The idea of the bereaved 'disengaging' with the deceased is a relatively modern and western concept and would be quite alien to our ancestors, and also to many other cultures.

Another problem with models of loss is that while they may reflect an amount of reality for adult mourning, they may not be transferable to the childhood experience. The three basic types of models of loss are shown below:

- the stage model of loss
- the task model of loss
- the continuing bonds model of loss.

The stage model perceives the bereaved as being relatively passive in terms of grieving. In contrast the task model perceives the bereaved individual as taking a more active role in moving through the grieving process, this through the completion of tasks. More recently the perspective of 'continuing bonds' and the idea that the bereaved individual has a continuing but changed relationship with the deceased has re-emerged as a model.

The stage model of loss

The stage model came from a research project involving terminally ill patients (Kübler-Ross 1982). These patients seemed to move through a series of stages from initially hearing that they were terminally ill. A typical response from the patients, on hearing the news that their illness was terminal, would be one of disbelief. The patients were in a state of shock and then tended to go into a denial mode. They could not accept what was happening and would 'pretend' or deny the reality. The patients would pass through various stages including the following:

- shock
- denial
- anger

- guilt
- depression
- resolution.

The patients eventually reached the stage of resolution and had come to terms with their fate. It was then suggested that the bereaved move through a similar series of stages after the death of someone close to them. At first there is a stage of shock and denial which gradually moves through to resolution, and the completion of mourning. The death does not then impact highly on the daily living of the bereaved, and they are now able to resume a large element of normality of living. The stages may not be in line with the ups and downs reported by many bereaved, where working through grief could be likened to riding sea-waves: there are calm as well as stormy times (Heegard 1991). A study of London widows introduced the notion of the fluidity of grieving, the bereaved passing through the stages of grief, but not necessarily in a fixed or in a rigid order, and they could well return to earlier stages of grieving before moving on to resolution (Parkes 1986). Children may have the need to come to terms with the death, then complete their grieving, finally resuming the progression towards the development of their personality (Furman 1974). Helping children through the initial stages is crucial, according to Furman.

The task model of loss

Bereavement can be seen as a series of tasks to work through, rather than just being a series of stages through which the individual has to pass (Worden 1984). Here, the bereaved plays an active rather than a passive role in the grieving process.

- The first task is to acknowledge their loss, and to accept the reality of the death.

- The second task is that of experiencing the pain of grief, perhaps both physical as well as emotional.
- The third task is to adjust to an environment without the deceased.
- The final task is to invest energy elsewhere, by withdrawing it from the deceased.

Children may work through four psychological tasks to complete their grieving (Fox 1991):

- understanding
- grieving
- commemorating
- moving on.

Children may also move through the stages of shock, denial, a growing awareness and finally acceptance of the death (Ward 1993). A potential problem with extending the adult models to children is that this assumes that their experiences of bereavement are similar.

The continuing bonds model of loss

The 'continuing bonds' model is a more recent grief model, although it does have historical echoes. The bereaved maintains links with the deceased: these bonds are not severed, but flow on into time (Silverman and Klass 1996). This does challenge the notion that grief can actually be resolved, in the sense of disengagement from the deceased. For many cultures in the world, the links between those alive and the dead 'ancestors' remain active and are fostered (Barnsley 1995). In Japanese culture, the ancestors 'remain' with the bereaved and the link with them is considered to be unbroken (Yamamoto 1970). It is interesting to compare the Mexican Day of the

Dead, where the ancestors are remembered and their graves are visited, with the eve of the Christian All Saints' Day, Hallowe'en, which involves a rather frightening 'celebration' of death and the 'supernatural', with ghouls and spooks, in sharp contrast with the Mexican celebrations.

Chapter 4

Schema theory and the importance of language

Schema theory

We are born without any apparent knowledge of our context and have to build an internal representation of the world through our encounters and interactions with the external. This is achieved through our senses and cognitive system and through the construction of internal models or schema, to represent the real world. Schema theory is top down processing and assumes that we have linked packages of expectations and concepts for things which we have encountered, for example we know what to expect at a picnic or a football match. We expect an outdoor event and sandwiches at a picnic, and a pitch, football and players at the football match. Models to represent our world are built up and for 'cognitive economy' we do not need them to make a detailed assessment of situations we have already previously encountered. One problem may be that our general 'death schema' may be inaccurately created through such external influences as the media. This exposure may not inoculate us against the experience of death, but could well increase our fear of it. Media death contrasts with first hand experience of the death of a parent, partner, child or close friend. Even if the death schema is correct in the media sense, it may not be transferable to the individual experience. It may though be a default perception, if we have no other data from our own experience to replace the media perspective. Children may well be acquiring models of the external world through the media to include such faulty schema.

The importance of language

Language is an important medium of communication through which we can also gain knowledge second hand. Because death can be taboo, adults tend to make use of euphemisms, which refer to the death in an indirect way. The use of euphemisms avoids mentioning the word 'death' directly and is intended to help to soften the impact of the word. Common euphemisms include 'passed away', 'gone to sleep', 'taken by Jesus' and 'kicked the bucket'. Euphemisms are normally well understood by adults. One difficulty is that euphemisms may confuse or even frighten children, if they take them literally. Some euphemisms are connected to belief systems, such as 'gone to heaven' or 'been taken by the angels'. However, even religious euphemisms have the potential to confuse children, who may think of heaven as a place from which you are able to return, like being on holiday, and may therefore expect the dead person to come back to visit them. Other euphemisms, such as 'kicked the bucket' or 'pushing up the daisies', may just confuse children with literal imagery relating to kicking buckets or pushing daisies. Euphemisms such as 'gone to sleep' may cause a child to be fearful of sleeping, and 'being taken by Jesus' could cause them to be afraid of going to church in case they were taken away. It seems important not to tell children things they will later have to unlearn, and in this context surely youngsters are best told the truth, at least in terms which they can understand (Grollman 1991). Children may not be able to understand medical terms such as a coronary, but they may understand that a heart has 'worn out'. Medical terminology can also be confusing; children may not understand how something as gentle as a 'stroke' can kill and how a heart can be 'attacked'. Care needs to be taken when giving explanations to children, especially younger ones and those with language difficulties or disorders. If children are not given explanations, they may fantasise about what has happened. Children may best be helped by being told the truth about a death and allowed to share their feelings with the other family members; misleading children may lead them to mistrust adults when they do find out the truth (LeShan 1979). Children need to be sensitively told the truth about death, although if adults generally feel uncomfortable in talking about death with other adults, then they may find the subject difficult to broach with children (Rinpoché 1992).

Chapter 5

Childhood bereavement and its effects

The frequency of loss

Many young people have the experience of a parent dying while they are at school. Around 3 per cent of the school population has experienced such a death, although not as many as the number who experience parental separation (CRUSE 1989). My own research in Humberside primary schools identified that over 70 per cent of schools had a recently bereaved child on roll (Holland 1993). These youngsters had experienced the death of a parent within the previous two years. My later research with Corinne Ludford made similar findings in the secondary phase of education (Holland and Ludford 1995). Around two-thirds of a sample of children in a secondary school had experienced the death of a 'close relative' (Branwhite 1994). The chances of a father dying are greater than that of a mother; 80 per cent of childhood parental deaths in one study were paternal (Ward 1994). This anomaly may relate to tendencies such as women marrying men older than themselves and also men dying at a younger age than women.

It therefore seems that there are likely to be a number of bereaved young people in any school, especially when the deaths of grandparents and other relations are included. If loss is broadened to include parental separation, then the number will increase even more. An irony is that, while schools and local authorities have 'disaster plans' in place for events that are unlikely to happen, such as an aircraft crashing onto the school, they may have nothing in place to react to the death of a parent of a child. Stirling Council, the local authority in which the Dunblane shootings took place, produced an emergency planning booklet, which also stressed the importance of schools having strategies in place for recognising and addressing 'normal' grief in children (Pickard 1999).

Short-term effects of bereavement for children

My previous research had shown that many bereaved children had short-term problems at school, and other research suggested that these difficulties could continue over a long time scale. Over nine out of ten children, in one study, showed some behaviour disturbances in the time immediately following their bereavement (Raphael 1982). The effects of both anger and depression were also noticed in my Humberside research, with children reported as having both behavioural and learning difficulties. In the educational sense, these children were achieving less than their potential, the death of the parent being a bar to their progress in learning, preventing the children from gaining full access to the curriculum. Schools may perceive bereaved children as having a pastoral rather than an educational special need. Children may experience a loss of concentration and focus after being bereaved, and this may affect their learning at school, leading to lower than potential attainments at school. Young people may be more prone to accidents after a parental death through their own preoccupation with grief, and consequent lack of concentration. Children may find the readjustments at home difficult to cope with, although paradoxically, some may immerse themselves in work, perhaps as a way of avoiding facing the reality of what has happened (Knapman 1993). The Humberside studies found that over three-quarters of primary schools having a recently bereaved child on roll noticed either a physical or a psychological post bereavement effect. In 40 per cent of schools, children were reported as being behaviourally disruptive, in terms of violence or anger, reflecting their grieving reactions. Crying was observed in 33 per cent of cases. Withdrawal, depression or moods was also reported in nearly 40 per cent of the children, this again reflecting grieving reactions. Over 30 per cent of the schools in the primary study reported children displaying symptoms of insecurity, such as overattachment or other obsessive behaviour. Significantly, about 30 per cent of the schools reported that children had shown either a marked lack of concentration or else suffered deterioration in their work at school. The results of the secondary phase study were similar to those in the primary sector, and the figures may well be an underestimate, as some things may go unnoticed or unconnected with the death. Aggression, at least in the classroom, may be quite apparent, but it may be less obvious when it occurs in the playground, in the school corridor, or on the way to and from school. Depression could also be perceived by teachers as children 'getting on with things', and as an overt sign of recovery. This could sharply contrast with the possible inner turmoil of the child. The perceptions of teachers too may change over time. There was a significant difference in reporting these effects between whether or not the school had a recently bereaved youngster on the roll. This may lie in the constructive memories of the teachers, rather than in the actual effects, as the bereavement recedes in time. One of the intentions of Iceberg was to investigate the short-term effects of the death of their parent on the volunteers taking part in the research.

Longer-term effects of bereavement for children

Adults seem to underestimate the amount of time which children may need to recover from and adjust to the imbalance in their lives caused by a major event in their life such as a death or parental separation. The effects of these losses, in terms of both learning and behaviour problems, may well extend into months and years rather than just days and weeks, especially without any support for the youngster.

Anecdotal evidence from some of my friends suggested that there were longer-term difficulties experienced by adults after the death of a parent during their childhood. Bereaved children may be more predisposed to clinging type behaviour in their subsequent life (Bowlby 1963). These longer-term difficulties included referral to the psychiatric services, for example in one study, some 60 per cent of single men committing suicide had suffered a maternal bereavement in the preceding three years (Bunch *et al.* 1971). Other studies found that some children who had been bereaved in adolescence tended to act 'out of character' after the death, including delinquent and other antisocial behaviour in the post bereavement phase (Shoor and Speed 1963). There seemed to be a negative shift in the behaviour of these bereaved children, perhaps an outward manifestation of their inner grieving and reflecting their anger towards society in general. There has been research making a direct link between adult mental illness, including schizophrenia and psychosis, and the childhood death of a parent (Ludford 1994). Bereaved children also tended to experience problems in their later life, for example in one study, female psychiatric patients bereaved before the age of 11 scored highly on measures of dependency, and tended to exhibit more neurotic type behaviour (Birtchnell 1975). In another study, 20 per cent of adolescents who had experienced the death of a parent scored within the major depression category of the Beck Depression Inventory, nearly thrice that reported in the general population (Gray 1989). Nearly half of the psychiatric patient admissions to a Dumfriesshire hospital had suffered the death of a parent within the previous 20 years, and 30 per cent of these were bereaved within the previous 10 years (Birtchnell 1970). Bereaved children were twice as likely to suffer a psychiatric disturbance in their adult life: 14 per cent of child referrals attending one child guidance clinic had recently been bereaved of a parent (Rutter 1966). There was a connection between the death of a parent when a child was between 3 and 4 years old and later disturbances in life. There was also a correlation between later adult depressive illness and the death of a parent between 10 and 14 years old (Hill 1969). Connections have been made between later adult drug abuse and unresolved childhood grief (Lamers 1986). The loss of a role model was perhaps a key factor, increasing the difficulties for children after parental death. A link has also been made between the death of a mother before her daughter was aged 11 and later adult depression (Brown, Harris and Copeland 1977). It may be that the childhood death of a mother can potentially lead to poor parenting, premarital and early pregnancy, as well as to depression in adulthood for some girls. Other children appeared to have both guilt and low self-esteem after a parental death, even where they later had significant academic or professional achievements (Mishne 1992). There seemed to be some quite problematic outcomes in later life for children who had been bereaved of a parent. The intention of Iceberg was to investigate further the longer-term effects on the volunteers taking part in the research.

Sex differences relating to bereavement

Some have found few gender differences between children after the death of a parent, although girls could generally share their feelings and felt more able to cry, whereas boys tended to feel that it was not socially acceptable for them to display uncontrolled feelings (Sanders 1995). This seems to reflect the adult experience, although, after a major tragedy, there was a higher proportion of problems among girls than with boys (Yule and Gold 1993). Emotions can cause changes in a girl's hormonal system, and the menstrual period may stop for a few months, an apparent physiological change induced by a psychological response to the death of a parent (Schaefer and Lyons 1986).

Chapter 6

How schools help bereaved children

Schools as supporters

Schools could potentially help bereaved young people through both a reactive and a proactive approach (Holland 1997). The reactive response ensures that children whose parent has died are helped through their initial grieving. This is emotional first aid, in order to minimise the risk of the children developing further difficulties and helping them to adjust to the new situation of their life. School is part of the social network and is therefore well placed to help to support the bereaved child. Some teenagers regarded school as a safe haven after both marital endings and bereavement, although the bereaved group felt they received less teacher support than did their peers experiencing a parental marital breakdown (Lewis 1992).

Teachers will do what they perceive to be the best to support their pupils at these times of crisis, but may lack the necessary skills. Teachers would seem to be important in terms of the emotional life of their pupils, and as such they could play a role in helping children (Leaman 1995). Children need a school environment in which well-being can be nurtured and the potential for damage hence minimised (Capewell 1994). It could also be argued that the role of the teacher is to be responsible for the pastoral welfare of the pupils in their care (Ludford 1994). An assumption being made here is that teachers have both the skills and the willingness to fulfil this role. The Humberside studies found that many teachers were neither adequately trained nor comfortable with the role of supporting bereaved children. Schools may not receive the same sort of support from other agencies, in the case of a parental bereavement, compared to where there has been a traumatic incident. The research suggests that schools generally do not have systems in place to react to the bereavement of their pupils. Schools seem to consider that bereavements are individual and need an individual response. While acknowledging this position, this does not preclude planning strategies and options before a death occurs (Holland 1997).

Schools could help children prepare for their future losses, by including the issue of loss and bereavement in the curriculum. This is a proactive approach, generally known as 'loss education', to help children through their feelings around little losses, as well as to help them to gain a greater understanding of the concept of death. This is intended to inoculate children, with the idea of improving how they cope with their own future losses and also to help foster communication between teachers and children. Death is an area affecting everyone and it could be contended that all young people should receive education in the area (Leaman 1995). If the issue is smoothly integrated into the curriculum, and mechanisms such as circle time or tutor time are used to explore feelings, then the barrier of the 'wall of silence' reported by many volunteers could be reduced. Loss education could relate to the numerous life changes experienced by children, such as parental separations, and the transitions which children make between classes, phases and schools. Nearly 80 per cent of teachers in Belfast primary schools thought that they had a part to play in helping children to develop an understanding in the area of death, although only 30 per cent of the school actively addressed death in the curriculum (Leckley 1991). This has echoes in the Humberside studies, with schools reporting on how highly they regarded the area, but in reality having little loss education in place. My own research found that loss is sometimes addressed by schools, but usually only on the initiative of an individual school, generally through an enthusiastic teacher.

In over half of schools, loss was addressed through the medium of religious education (RE), with a focus on cross-cultural and religious issues. Death education also took place in other areas of the curriculum, such as English. Both RE and English may actually distance pupils from their own emotional experiences. Learning about funeral rites in faraway cultures or the poems of the First World War will be unlikely to engage with youngsters' own experiences of life and is not really related to their own feelings.

Another issue for teachers is the availability of time in the curriculum: schools already have a high level of curriculum and performance pressure. Teachers are obliged to address a range of specific areas, as defined in the National Curriculum, and may not have time to become skilled in the area of loss, grief and death education.

Schools may have neither the resources nor the skills to cope with the grieving child in a reactive manner, and be even less able to prepare children in a proactive manner for bereavement, through loss or death education in the curriculum. Teachers may be reluctant to discuss a parental death with a bereaved child. They may feel that this would bridge the professional relationship they have with the youngster, to become a relationship involving discussion of a particularly personal and sensitive nature (Abrams 1993). Teachers may address the issue of death and bereavement at arm's length, removing the emotional element (Rowling 1994). Teachers may have difficulty with death through their own unresolved problems perhaps hindering them from helping bereaved children (Sisterton 1983). Some teachers may have 'disenfranchised grief', being neither fully acknowledged nor socially supported and relating to the general cultural context in England (Rowling 1995). Teachers may also hold back from approaching the child, not wishing to broach the subject of the death, through the fear of causing 'upset'. Teachers need to be comfortable with the grieving process, as well as facing their own feelings about death, before they are able to support their bereaved pupils effectively (Martin 1983). Another intention of Iceberg was to investigate how schools, teachers and others could support children in the future, through the experiences of the volunteers taking part in the research.

Teacher training in loss and bereavement

Some researchers have emphasised the need for teachers to receive training in the area of bereavement (Rowling 1994). Primary school teachers may lack initial teacher training in personal and social education and counselling (Charlton and Hoye 1987). The Humberside research supported this view: only a very few teachers had received any training in the area of loss, most had received none. The primary school research in Humberside and the secondary schools in the follow-up study identified that schools thought that more training and resources were needed. On a more positive note, after receiving in-service training, teachers tend to become more confident in talking to and helping bereaved children in their schools (Urbanowicz 1994).

Many classroom teachers may be relatively young, perhaps lacking in life experience, and unless they themselves have been through a close bereavement, they may not be able to empathise easily with children who have experienced the death of a parent.

Teachers will be likely to grow in confidence in dealing with the issue of loss, death and bereavement only if they receive training, in particular in relation to the experience and understanding of death by children. A frequent comment by the Iceberg volunteers was that teachers could better help bereaved children if this area was more explicitly addressed either in teacher training or by post qualification courses. In the Humberside research, schools also expressed the need for this additional training. The Learning Services Directorate of Kingston upon Hull City Council addressed this need through the training package 'Lost for Words'. This is a basic 'loss awareness' training package that can be delivered by suitable trainers directly into schools. Teachers do need to be empowered in the area of loss and death, and not to perceive it as one for the expert. At some times it may be prudent to involve outside agencies to help to support a bereaved child, but most could be helped, with an increase in teacher knowledge and confidence in their own abilities to relate to bereaved children on a human level. The involvement of outside agencies, although perhaps necessary in a small minority of cases, reinforces the message that death is an unusual event which teachers cannot cope with.

Support for the child at home

Bereaved children may receive little support for their bereavement at school, in terms of either proactive loss education or reactive support after a death. Youngsters may also have little support at home, where the adults may be working through their own grief, and be distracted as to the needs of the child. There is evidence suggesting that the care of children may suffer after the death of a parent, for example it has been estimated that there is a 30 per cent reduction in the daily care of pre-school children (Kranzler *et al.* 1990). The adults in the child's family may not be in a position fully to appreciate that the bereaved children too need to mourn. It may be that it is the grief of the surviving parent rather than the sorrow of the children that is likely to dominate the household (Wolff 1992). Parents may also underestimate the effect that the bereavement is having on the youngsters (Weller *et al.* 1988). Even if the adult family members do recognise and acknowledge the need of the bereaved children to grieve, they may still be unable to facilitate the children's grieving. With the best of intentions, adults may seek to protect children from contact with the death, through the use of euphemisms or by avoiding the topic.

It seems important that children are involved with things after a death in the family, with others being open to them about events (Kubler-Ross 1991). Adults need to help the children in relation to their thoughts and feelings about the bereavement and it is only then that they are able to move forwards to resolve their grief. From the perception of the bereaved child, it may be that they seek to protect the surviving parent and other adults, by containing or repressing their own grief. There is evidence that adolescents tended not to confide in their parents during the first year after the death of a sibling (Balk 1983). There would seem to be difficulties for both parents and children in the post bereavement period, with the danger that the grieving of children is not facilitated. Bereaved child may 'mark time' in their grieving until an adult facilitates them (Raphael 1984). The children may be caught in 'frozen blocks of time' and may not be able to break free without the support of adult grief work (Goldman 1996). If these bereaved children are unable to communicate their grief, then it may be that they are laying the foundations of future problems for themselves. The bereaved child with unresolved issues may become a poor role model for their own children. Adolescents seem particularly vulnerable to the danger of their grief becoming pathologised if it is not facilitated. Children face the loss and protection of the adult world through the death of a parent or carer (Alder 1994). The biggest fear children may have after bereavement is that of being deserted, or that the surviving parent may die, which may only compound their insecurity (Kubler-Ross 1983). Children may experience grief in a different way from adults, as pockets of intermittent intense and profound involvement and making particular use of denial and fantasy (Hemmings 1995).

Communication links

The speedy establishment of good communications between the school and the surviving parent seems important. It needs to be remembered that the surviving parent will probably be deeply affected by the death of their partner. Effective communications should bring benefits for bereaved children.

> Pamela said that her close-knit primary school had responded well and sensitively to the death of her father, and that this helped to support her through the difficult times. Pamela's perception was that the school really cared about the death of her father and the impact it had on her and her family.

The involvement of the school after the death, such as by sending flowers to a funeral, or even someone attending if that was felt to be appropriate, would give an overt acknowledgement of the death to the children. This should help to reduce their isolation, and could also increase the chances that they would approach teachers for help or just to talk things through with them. Potentially teachers could also help the surviving parent with decisions such as whether to involve the children in the post death rites. Teachers could discuss with parents the potential problems of not involving children in the rituals and could discuss the issues of control, power and understanding. My own experience of working with newly bereaved adults is that they would welcome help in this area. Teachers could also warn the surviving parents about the danger of children becoming isolated and having no one to talk with about the experience.

Chapter 7

Children's understanding of and interest in death

Children's understanding of death

Adults may consider that children do not have a real under-standing of death, which may lead them to take the view that children do not need to grieve or to become involved in the rites after a death. There is evidence that suggests the opposite is the case. Research on attachment and separation showed that babies notice their separation from the person providing the main care (Bowlby 1973). By early school age, many children may have begun to grasp a basic concept of death, in particular its meaning and fear (Zach 1978). By 3 years old, many children will have gained the realisation of death; the average 6-year-old child would have grasped the concept that death is irreversible (Kane 1979). Children may have some confused notions as to what death entails and wonder, for example, how the dead go to the toilet, or eat their food. By the time most youngsters reach the age of 12 years, they will probably have an understanding of death close to that of an adult. The gradual acquisition of the concept of death fits in with the theories of Piaget (1929). In Piagetian theory, children move from an animist or a magical thinking stage through to the stage of formal operations and later to that of abstract thought (Lovell 1973). It is perhaps not coincidental that children seem to achieve an adult concept of death at a similar time that they achieve a more sophisticated way of thinking (Wass and Corr 1984). The Vygotskian notion of the zone of proximal development, another social constructivist theory, also fits in here. This includes 'scaffolding' and the idea of children gradually building up their knowledge of death through both the experience and guidance from adults, in both a formal and informal way (Van der Veer and Valsiner 1994). The adults, including the teachers of bereaved children, may not realise how much they understand, and there may be a mismatch between the perceptions of bereaved children and their teachers (Blackburn 1991). It was also intended to investigate children's understanding of death through the experiences of the Iceberg volunteers taking part in the research.

Children's interest in death

Children may have a far greater interest and knowledge about death than many adults realise – witness such playground games like 'bang bang you're dead!' – and 3–5-year-old children do think a lot about death (Rochlin 1967). It is not clear as to how children obtain their information about death, since there seems to be little direct education, and a tendency for adults not to engage with them in the topic. Children will encounter media deaths, especially those on television, from an early age and they cannot in reality be sheltered from this exposure (Kastenbaum 1974). Some of the information children glean may be highly inaccurate, and gained through a process of Chinese Whispers, such as in the playground and from their peers. Death may even be part of the adolescent culture and experience, especially with the spectre of Acquired Immune Deficiency Syndrome (AIDS) and other death related themes often found in adolescent music (Corr 1991). Examples of such music include 'Die young, stay pretty' by Blondie (1979), 'Stairway to heaven' by Led Zeppelin (1971), 'A hard rain's gonna fall' by Bob Dylan (1963) and 'The way friends do' by Abba (1981). The song recorded by Mike and the Mechanics (1988), 'The living years', relates to paternal death.

Chapter 8

The background to Iceberg

Introduction

My previous research in Humberside was with teachers and schools, and not directly with bereaved children. The idea of Iceberg was to interview individuals about their experiences after the death of a parent when they were children. This was to gain an insight into their experiences, especially at school and with the idea of using this information to help to improve the support for currently bereaved children. Iceberg was carried out under the auspices of the University of York: I thought that it was important for credibility that it was scrutinised and subject to academic rigour.

The research questions

Iceberg sought to answer four research questions:

1. What is the experience of parental death like for children, in terms of their grieving, power, and the support, facilitation or otherwise they receive from their family and school?

2. How can adults, in particular teachers, give effective support for bereaved children at school, what helps and what hinders the grieving process?

3. Is the issue of loss and bereavement addressed by schools, and if so is it done in a meaningful way, i.e.

does it have positive outcomes in terms of helping children?

4.   How does the experience of bereavement affect children in the short, medium and long term? Are they more likely to have time off school, through illness, as an indirect effect of unresolved grief?

The research method

Research in a sensitive subject such as death, especially with children, presents ethical difficulties and I considered several methods of research for Iceberg. The experimental method was discarded as not being appropriate. Iceberg was a trawl for information, which could lead to revised perceptions within the area of childhood parental bereavement. An experimental approach, with tightly controlled variables, was not practical. The experimental method could dehumanise and distort behaviour, and not provide a true picture (Dobson *et al.* 1981). Participatory or non-participatory observation was considered, but it would have been both difficult and time-consuming to organise, as well as potentially affecting behaviour. This would have involved observing children and their family at a time of crisis, after a death, and would have been obtrusive, with the potential to cause offence, even if any family were willing to consent to such intrusion on their grief. This may have been the best way to gain the clearest picture, as direct observations could be made at the time, although these observations could be a subjective interpretation of the events taking place (Bannister *et al.* 1994).

Discarding the experimental and observation methods, a survey approach seemed to be more appropriate, such as by interviews or questionnaires. Surveys are appropriate as a method of investigation when people are willing to self-report. The crux of Iceberg was around the experiences of children bereaved of a parent when they were of school age. The most direct way of finding out about their experiences and the effects on the children at the time of the death seemed to be obvious, that was to ask them! An interview is a two-person conversation initiated by the interviewer for the purpose of obtaining relevant research information (Cannell and Kahn 1968). It is a direct verbal interaction, a special form of conversation, in contrast to a questionnaire where volunteers make their own written responses.

One difficulty is that volunteers may not be truthful, and even if they are truthful, they may not fully understand a question, misinterpret it, or answer in a way to try and please the researcher. Even if volunteers intend to be open and honest, there could be distortions caused by the lapse of time, although this is specifically addressed later. The less structured the interview, the more likely that information would be genuinely given and that it would be both richer and fuller (Coolican 1994). The balance of power between the researcher and the volunteer is perhaps more equal, the less structured is the interview, and by so empowering volunteers the data may be richer. A compromise between an open-ended interview and a questionnaire is a semi-structured interview, where a questionnaire sheet is used as a framework for an interview, but the volunteer is able to expand on information, the researcher guiding the interview through the various areas. This type of survey also enables the researcher to collect any additional information, to observe non-verbal communication, and to follow a particular line of inquiry if appropriate.

The use of interviews brings with it problems of potential interviewer bias. I had concerns that schools may not be as effective as possible in supporting childhood bereavement. There was the danger of my transferring this bias to the volunteers, who may then present a distorted picture of their reality. There is always the potential for influences between the researcher and the respondent, and it would be unrealistic to assume that there can ever be a position of total neutrality (Guba and Lincoln 1987). The importance is an awareness of such issues, and an attempt to minimise, rather than to pretend that they do not exist. With regard to whether volunteers would be truthful, it is not possible to ensure that anybody tells the truth, although there would seem to be no obvious motivation in the volunteers misleading me. It was decided that the research would be partly by semi-structured interview, and partly by questionnaire, an interview by proxy, and as such it seemed reasonable to have both methods in the study (Walker 1989).

The Iceberg volunteers

Iceberg was a retrospective study, as the bereaved children were not actually interviewed until they were adults, and also not before at least five years had elapsed after the death of their parent. The time scale was to enable the volunteers to reflect on their experiences over time, and also to avoid as far as possible interfering with the normal process of grieving. Interviewing children after a parental death involved too many difficulties, especially as they were not really in a position to give informed consent.

Volunteers were obtained for Iceberg through both 'opportunity' and 'snowball' sampling. The opportunity contacts were those initial contacts I had already made through various means, and snowballing relates to the subsequent contacts that developed from the originals. The use of snowball sampling, or networking, allows the researcher to gain access to a particular group (Lee 1993). Iceberg was essentially 'qualitative' in nature, the emphasis being on meanings and experiences, although the volunteers were asked to rate some of their experiences on a number scale.

Ethics

Death is a sensitive topic raising ethical issues for research. 'Good and right' are basic principles of ethics (Tschudin and Marks-Maran 1992). Guidance was also given by the World Medical Assembly's (1964) declaration of Helsinki. Ethical concerns include the non-abuse of volunteers, where there is a difference in power, such as between researcher and volunteers. The researcher is in control of the situation, the latter potentially having little power. In Iceberg the volunteers were all interviewed at the place of their choice, in their own home or territory, in an attempt to keep the balance of power between myself and the volunteer as equal as possible. Additional precautions were taken to preserve the anonymity of the volunteers taking part in Iceberg. The tapes used to record the interviews were erased, and the names used in the book have been changed to avoid volunteers being identified – the randomised naming means that more than one name may represent an individual.

Memory

There is evidence from eyewitness testimony suggesting that individuals do have constructed memories, and that they may well recall past memories inaccurately, bringing their own prejudices and mind-sets into their memories (Loftus 1975). This is similar to the game of Chinese Whispers, where individuals rearrange and modify memories in order for them to make sense. Individuals tend to recall events in line with their own stereotypic schema assumptions or previous knowledge (Bartlett 1932). Until a death occurs, a youngster would probably have only a very flimsy schema regarding the area of death, usually obtained from the media or the playground. The event of the death may then lead to the creation of a 'parent dying' schema which will then stand on its own and may not be absorbed into another schema nor modified. Evidence from cognitive psychology would tend to support the view that bereaved children can have an accurate recall of events. Memories of President John F. Kennedy's assassination have been investigated, and many of the volunteers interviewed also had quite vivid or 'flashbulb' memories of where they were and what they were doing at the actual time when they heard the news of their parent's death. The news of the death was equally as suprising as the news of the JFK assassination (Brown and Kulick 1982). This had a high impact, such as to trigger neural mechanisms which helped the volunteers to retain the memories over the long term. An alternative explanation could be that such memories were well retained by individuals because of their high impact and because there was frequent reconsideration and rehearsal after the event (Neisser 1982). This kept the recall of events highly accurate over a long time period. Flashbulb memories may be no different from any other vivid memories, relating to events that make an impact, such as encounters with the opposite sex and accidents (Rubin and Kozin 1984). The parental death may make such an emotional impact that the memory is retained as episodic rather than being converted to semantic memory (Tulving 1972). This suggests that the memories of individuals around an event, such as the death of a parent, may be both vivid and accurate despite the passage of time.

Obtaining the Iceberg volunteers

Although I already had contact with several people willing to be interviewed for Iceberg, these were insufficient in number and a 'wave strategy' was used in the search for volunteers. This involved working through the following strategies until enough volunteers were obtained:

- personal contacts with friends and their friends
- personal contacts with a local counselling organisation
- contacting by letter all the local bereavement counselling organisations
- placing an advertisement in the *Times Educational Supplement*, asking for volunteers
- talking about Iceberg on a local radio station
- appealing in the local education bulletin sent weekly to local schools
- advertising in *SESAME*, the Open University student publication.

I eventually obtained 70 adult volunteers who fitted the criteria of having a parent die when they were of school age, and also having at least five years elapse since the death. The interviews took place mainly, although not exclusively, within the Humberside, Yorkshire, Lincolnshire and East Anglia areas of England. Those volunteers who responded by questionnaires were located nationwide.

The Iceberg volunteers who I interviewed, without exception, felt positive after the experience. For some the interview seemed to have been a cathartic experience and they welcomed the opportunity to talk to somebody about a significant event in their life. There was a tendency, reflected in both the interviews and the questionnaires, for volunteers to feel very positive about Iceberg and the aim of helping future bereaved children. If anything, the Iceberg volunteers felt that they were helping to turn what had been a negative life event for them to a positive way of helping future children.

Analysis of the Iceberg data

I completed the gathering of information for Iceberg in the autumn of 1996, and the interview schedules are shown in the appendices. Although some interest in Iceberg did continue after that time, it was not overwhelming, and I had ceased seeking more contacts. A large amount of data was obtained from the Iceberg volunteers and this was then analysed. Travelling for the interviews was quite a time-consuming activity, although very enjoyable in terms of meeting with and interviewing the volunteers. The analysis of the data was both time-consuming and laborious. There are three main tasks in checking either interview schedules or self-completed questionnaires (Moser and Kalton 1977).

The first task relates to completeness, checking that all the questions had been answered. This task was completed quickly, and there were no difficulties because there had been responses to all the questions.

The second task is to check that all the questions were answered accurately. This was a difficult task, although I did check the schedules for consistency. I had to rely on the volunteers being honest, and also having a large degree of self-awareness about their experience, as well as having had time to reflect on their experiences.

The third task is to ensure continuity between the interviewers. This did not apply, as I was the only interviewer. The analysing of closed questions was not as difficult as analysing the open questions with discourse. The open-ended questions needed a more subjective analysis of the content of the data.

The closed questions were analysed by calculating the totals and scores given in answers. Where the data were scores, the mean, mode, median and range were also calculated.

The analysis of the open questions was far more complex and demanding. The first task of reducing the data to a more manageable amount was by coding (Cohen and Manion 1994). The open-ended questions were not pre-coded before the data collection, as it had not been possible to predict what answers would be given by the volunteers. The coding of the data involved an initial scan of all the data sheets, with the identification of key words and phrases. The schedules were rescrutinised, and a tally made of the key words and phrases. These were then recorded onto a summary data sheet, and recorded in the various tables.

The information obtained from the Iceberg volunteers was divided into five age ranges, relating to the age of the volunteers at the time of the death of their parent:

- pre-school
- infant school
- junior school
- younger secondary school
- older secondary school

The information was also categorised by the sex of the parent dying, by the sex of the volunteer, and whether the death was sudden or anticipated.

Validity

An aim of social science is to produce descriptions and explanations of the social world, which involves efforts to ensure both accuracy and truthfulness. Reliability relates to the accuracy of the measures used in the research while validity involves whether the instrument used actually measures what is intended. Volunteers may seek to mislead researchers, a potential flaw with any research, although it was hoped to minimise this through using face-to-face interviews and having close contact with those submitting questionnaires. There was also quite a large sample, which should dilute any element of misleading, as there may be general patterns emerging. There also seemed to be no real incentive for volunteers to mislead me, rather they had an opportunity to retell their story. Many of the Iceberg volunteers expressed empathy with contemporary bereaved children and seemed to have the incentive to relate their experiences honestly. There is no absolute objective truth, but each of us will make sense of events in terms of how we construe them (Kelly 1955). We all have our own reality and the transmission of this to another does need clear communication from both the listener and speaker. Volunteers may avoid fully answering questions which they considered were 'too deep', and their story may have been related only in part. I attempted to minimise these difficulties through the procedures, using clear language for the questions, as well as coming to the research with the intended stance of neutrality. It is unrealistic to assume that there can ever be a position of total neutrality (Guba and Lincoln 1987). The importance is an awareness of the difficult issues, and an attempt to minimise them, rather than to pretend they do not exist.

The coding of the Iceberg volunteers' statements into the broad categories was a potential weakness in the link. Key words and meanings were used in this process, but there may well have been misunderstandings, even with the best will of the volunteers. This stage of Iceberg was the most laborious, as the coding of the data was checked, rechecked and balanced. This did take away some of the richness of each individual's story, although it enabled me to make some cumulative gener-alisations about the experiences of the volunteers as a group. It would not have been possible to relate the stories of the 70 vol-unteers in a case study approach.

Chapter 9

Introduction to the results

The Iceberg volunteers

Nearly 100 volunteers took part in Iceberg: 70 volunteers who had been bereaved of a parent when they were of school age took part in the project, as did a small number of the surviving parents and teachers of such bereaved children. The majority of the volunteers lived in eastern England, in the area from Humberside and Yorkshire through to Lincolnshire and East Anglia, although there were representatives from most parts of the country.

Of the volunteers 64 per cent were female and 36 per cent were male. This difference may have been because women are more willing to volunteer, or that they are more willing to share their experiences in this type of sensitive area. Perhaps women were more likely to have been targeted through the strategies I used to obtain volunteers. There tend to be more females involved in counselling and perhaps they were also more likely to read the personal columns of the publications in which the advertisements were placed or to be students of the Open University. The subjects were aged from 18 years old to 61 years old, the age range for males being 19–55, females 18–61. The median age for males was 32 years and for females 35 years. The range of time from bereavement was from 5 to 52 years – males 5–48, females 7–52 – while the median time since death was 25 years for males and 26 years for females.

Of the parental deaths 32 per cent were of mothers and 68 per cent were of fathers. The greater percentage of fathers in

Iceberg reflected that children do experience more paternal than maternal deaths (Ward 1994). While 56 per cent of the parental deaths were sudden, 44 per cent were anticipated. There are no national figures comparing sudden and anticipated deaths, although roughly 50 per cent more males than females do die in accidents (Office for National Statistics 1997). Deaths are recorded by nature, but there are too many ambiguities to be clear whether deaths are anticipated or sudden.

About 60 per cent of paternal deaths were sudden, compared to 45 per cent of the maternal deaths. There were no significant sex differences between the parental deaths in road traffic accidents or in suicide, although only fathers died through heart attacks or fights. These differences seem to reflect the greater risk of men in this age group being involved in these events.

The data tables

The results are shown categorised by the age groups of the volunteers at the time of the death of their parent:

- Less than 5 years old (pre-school)
- 5–7 years old (infant school)
- 8–11 years old (junior school)
- 12–15 years old (younger secondary school)
- 16 years and over (older secondary school)

Table 9.1 summarises all the Iceberg volunteers, Table 9.2 shows the female volunteers and Table 9.3 the male volunteers.

Table 9.1 Summary of the Iceberg volunteers

	Pre-school		5–7 yr		8–11 yr		12–15 yr		16+ yr		Totals		
	Mum	Dad	Mum	Dad	Mum	Dad	Mum	Dad	Mum	Dad	Mum	Dad	Total
Not sudden death		1	1	2	6	7	5	7		2	12	19	31
Sudden death		4	2	3	4	8	4	11		3	10	29	39
Total		5	3	5	10	15	9	18		5	22	48	70

Table 9.2 Summary of the female Iceberg volunteers

	Pre-school		5–7 yr		8–11 yr		12–15 yr		16+ yr		Totals		
	Mum	Dad	Mum	Dad	Mum	Dad	Mum	Dad	Mum	Dad	Mum	Dad	Total
Not sudden death		1		1	5	3	4	6		1	9	12	21
Sudden death		3	1		2	7	3	6		2	6	18	24
Total		4	1	1	7	10	7	12		3	15	30	45

Table 9.3 Summary of the male Iceberg volunteers

	Pre-school		5–7 yr		8–11 yr		12–15 yr		16+ yr		Totals		
	Mum	Dad	Mum	Dad	Mum	Dad	Mum	Dad	Mum	Dad	Mum	Dad	Total
Not sudden death			1	1	1	4	1	1		1	3	7	10
Sudden death		1	1	3	2	1	1	5		1	4	11	15
Total		1	2	4	3	5	2	6		2	7	18	25

There were no great sex differences between the volunteers in terms of the general patterns, except that all the parental deaths of the pre-school and the 16-plus age groups were of fathers. There were five bereavements in the pre-school group, eight in the infant age group, twenty-five bereavements in the junior age group, twenty-seven in the younger secondary age group, and five in the older secondary age group.

Chapter 10

The first reactions to the death

Introduction

Iceberg charted the experiences of the volunteers over time, from the initial news of the death of their parent to the longer-term effect the death had on their lives. This chapter relates the volunteers' stories for the first three weeks immediately after the death of the parent. This period includes the initial reaction of the volunteers to the news of the death of their parent, their involvement in the rites and rituals after the death, and their first return to school.

The first reactions on hearing the news of the death

Table 10.1 shows the reports of the Iceberg volunteers when they first heard the news of the death of their parent.

The most common responses reported by volunteers were those of 'disbelief' and feeling 'numbed', each being reported by nearly one-third of the volunteers. This suggests that the Iceberg volunteers, when they were children, had not fully absorbed the reality of the death. There is a difference between 'disbelief' – that is, not initially believing what had happened – and 'numbed' – indicating an inability to respond to the event. Nearly two-thirds of the Iceberg volunteers reported either 'disbelief' or 'numbed' as an initial response to the news

Table 10.1 The volunteers' first reactions to the news of the death of their parent	
Reaction	%
Disbelief	31
Numbed	27
Tears	13
Shock	13
Relief	13
No recall	11
Fear	10
Sadness	9
Guilt	7
Why me?	6
Embarrassed	6
Anger	4
Lost/alone	4
Premonition	4

of the death of their parent. Other volunteers described being 'shocked' and feeling that the news was 'unreal'.

It is not surprising that children's initial reaction to the death of a parent is one of shock, since even where the death is anticipated a familiar figure in their life has been suddenly removed. Shock is a common initial reaction for both adults and children.

Three-quarters of the Iceberg volunteers reported reactions indicating either an initial inability to absorb the news fully or failure to respond to the information of the death of their parent. One in eight of the Iceberg volunteers said that they were tearful on first hearing the news of the death, and just under one in eleven said that they felt sad. One in fourteen of the volunteers reported feeling guilt as an initial response: this is generally considered to be a much later reaction in the adult models of grief. One in nine of the volunteers reported that they had no recall of hearing the news of the death; these were all in the lowest three age groups when they were bereaved, including over half of the pre-schoolers.

When the volunteers reporting that they had 'no recall' of the events around hearing the news were discounted, the 'none absorbing' group rose to over 80 per cent of the volunteers. This was quite a high percentage of the volunteers who did not really fully take in what was happening at the time of their parent's death. One in eight of the Iceberg volunteers said that they felt relief after the death of their parent. This related mainly to the relief that the ordeal of their parent suffering had ended after a long illness. Three-quarters of these reports were made by female volunteers and all concerned their mothers:

> Mary was a teenager at the time of her mother's death, and she told how she found the experience of watching her mother's suffering during her terminal illness very difficult to bear. This suffering continued over many months, as her mother became increasingly incapacitated and dependent on others for all her needs. When eventually Mary's mother did die, Mary's feelings were of relief as the ordeal which she felt her mother had suffered had finished.

In contrast, the male volunteers reported these initial 'relief' responses only after the death of their fathers:

> Adrian was of junior school age at the time of his father's death and he reported that his response to the news of the death of his father was one of relief that it was not his mum who had died. Adrian seemed to have had a much closer relationship with his mother than he did with his father.

Craig was 10 years old at the time of his father's death and he reported relief on hearing the news. Craig was glad that his dad was now dead, as he could no longer physically abuse him. This was a sad story of a father who would use quite heavy physical discipline against his young son.

The female volunteers' relief in Iceberg seemed to be based on compassion, and the relief that the suffering had ended for the parent, and also for the child. Some of the volunteers had seen their parents experience quite painful illnesses. In contrast, the male volunteers' relief in Iceberg seemed to be related to their own self-interest, as with Adrian and Craig. None of these Iceberg volunteers reported any subsequent later feelings of guilt after their initial feelings of relief.

A very small group of the Iceberg volunteers reported having had premonitions of the death of their parent. These were mainly where fathers had died suddenly. When asked if they could explain further, the volunteers said that they 'just knew' what had happened to their father before they were actually told. One related to the period from when the parent first became diagnosed with a terminal illness, and this did seem to help in terms of preparing for the death. It is always difficult to tease out these types of premonitions. Their premonitions may have related to the initial reactions of the adults around the children, perhaps having very negative non-verbal communication, and giving hints that something extremely dreadful had happened, although not initially revealing the news of the death. These volunteers may also have been anxious as children, perhaps always tending to fear and anticipate the worst. As with the reported feelings of relief, I have encountered adults, in the context of bereavement counselling, who have had similar premonitions of the death of a close individual, and these reports should not be too easily discounted, and are perhaps an area worthy of more investigation.

Another small group of Iceberg volunteers reported feeling embarrassed by being 'different' on hearing the news of the death. These were all females of various ages at the time of the death, and there was no difference whether the death was of the mother or father. Death has the propensity to cause embarrassment and it may have been that the children were also reflecting the feelings of the adults around them (Golding 1991). A similar small group of female volunteers reported feelings of fear on hearing the news of the death of their parent:

> Vicki was 9 when her mum died and she told how she felt quite fearful when her mum died, thinking that her dad would not now be able to cope with everything on his own.

Other female volunteers said that they fainted, screamed or felt sick on hearing the news; none of these types of reactions were reported by any of the male volunteers. One female volunteer who was in junior school was told later that she screamed for about five minutes, and then never spoke or asked about what was happening.

There was a small group of males who reported having an anger response, others that they laughed on hearing the news of the death, suggesting that they had not absorbed the full impact of the news; this is also not an uncommon reaction for adults.

> Trevor was a young teenager, and on hearing the news of his father's death he said that he just shouted at the top of his voice, and then just ran and ran, he just had to run.

There was a slight sex difference between the initial responses of the volunteers, fear being reported by only the females and anger reported by only males. The results generally fit in with the adult models of grieving, suggesting that a large proportion of the volunteers, as children, had a similar initial reaction to adults on hearing the news of the death of someone close to them. The stage models have the responses of 'shock' or 'denial' as initial stages and the task model has an initial task of 'accepting the reality of the death'. The initial reactions of the Iceberg volunteers to the death of their parent does seem to mirror the adult experience quite closely. Table 10.2 summarises the reactions of the volunteers to hearing the news of the death of their parent.

Table 10.2 Summary of the volunteers' main initial reactions to the death		
General reaction	Percentage 1	Percentage 2
Information not fully absorbed	73	82
Tears/sadness	22	25
Relief	13	15
Fear	10	11
Anger	4	5
No recall	11	N/A

The 'percentage 1' figure in Table 10.2 is based on the total volunteer pool. A minority of the Iceberg volunteers could not recall their first reactions to the news of the death of their parent, and the 'percentage 2' figure is when the 'no recall' group were removed. The 'information not absorbed' group of volunteers then rises to over 80 per cent.

All the Iceberg volunteers in the two oldest age groups were able to recall their reactions. In the younger age groups, there was an inverse relationship between the age of the volunteers and the percentage able to recall events. About 66 per cent of the pre-school group, 40 per cent of the infant group and just under 10 per cent of the junior aged group were unable to recall events. An interesting feature was that in all of the instances except one, when Iceberg volunteers could not recall the events around the time of the death, this was the death of their father. There were twenty-five paternal and thirteen maternal deaths in the first three age groups, and this was a significant difference in the rate of recall. This suggests that the death of a mother may have had a greater impact on the young child than the death of a father. This could relate to bonding and attachment as well as to the potential impact on the daily living routine, all perhaps having more focus on the mother than on the father for the younger age groups. The suddenness of the death had no effect on the volunteers' ability to recall the events. The percentage of sudden as opposed to anticipated deaths in the 'no recall' group was within 1 per cent of the total sample. One volunteer thought that he may have blanked out memories from that time because they were so painful.

Breaking such news as the death of a parent is probably very difficult for both the teller and the receiver. The Iceberg volunteers were all children at the time of the death of their parent, and were told the news of the death by adults having control of when and how to deliver the news. Despite this adult control, some volunteers were told the news of the death in far from ideal circumstances:

> Thomas was 13 years old at the time of his father's sudden death. He was told of the death by the headmaster of his school, a man he said that he did not really know. Thomas was withdrawn from his class, shown into the headmaster's office, and then just told that his father had died. He was told to keep a 'stiff upper lip' and then sent back to his class to carry on with his lesson.

> Judith was in her late teens when her mother died, and she was simply told by her aunt that 'your mother died this afternoon'.

Most of the Iceberg volunteers were told in a far more supportive way than Judith or Thomas. It is hard to understand why
Thomas had not been offered some degree of support, even
just to sit down with a hot drink. Thomas, on reflection as an
adult, thought that for some unknown reason the headmaster
had been given the task of telling him the news of the death.
The headmaster seemed quite uncomfortable with this role,
and was able only to blurt out the news to Thomas and then
quickly send him back to his class. Thomas would have pre-
ferred to have heard the news from somebody better known to
himself, ideally his mother, and also have been given time to
absorb the news, preferably returning home at once rather
than carrying on with his lessons as if nothing had happened.
It may have been the same with Judith's aunt, who perhaps just
did not know how to tell the youngster.

The reports of the Iceberg volunteers also emphasise the
importance of who and how children are told of bad news,
such as the death of a parent. Ideally schools should have given
some thought as to how to respond if this happens to a pupil.
In a small number of instances, circumstances were such that
volunteers were themselves told by an sibling or even had the
task of breaking the news of the death to the surviving parent:

> Aged 16 at the time of his father's death, Kenneth was told
> the news of the death over the phone, and was so shocked
> that he asked a friend to phone for confirmation. Hardly
> surprisingly, Kenneth dreaded having the task of telling his
> mother.

> Julie was 13 at the time of her father's death at home after a
> long illness, and she was the person who found him after he
> had died. Julie described the feelings of disbelief and reali-
> sation that immobilised her after the event.

The Iceberg volunteers' understanding of what was happening at the time of the death

The volunteers were next asked if they understood what was happening at the time of their parent's death and there were two main responses. Nearly half of the Iceberg volunteers said that they did understand what was happening at the time of the death. One-third of the volunteers said that they did not understand what was happening at the time of the death.

Just over half of the volunteers said they did not *fully* understand what was happening at the time of the death. Another tenth of the volunteers said that they were given quite confusing information at the time of the death. Yet another tenth of the volunteers said that they did not fully grasp things or that they had only a vague recall of the events at the time.

Some volunteers were not told the truth of what was happening at the time of the death, or else they were given false hope that things would be all right if, for example, their parent was in hospital:

> Lisa was 9 years old at the time of her mother's death. She had been told at the time that her mother was going into hospital for a routine operation and that there was nothing to worry about. This was not at all the case: the operation was actually an emergency, and her mother had only a limited chance of survival.

Lisa was not told the true reason for the operation, nor was she given any hint that there could be complications. This was despite the fact, as she later found out, that the operation had only a small chance of being successful. With hindsight Lisa had been given no opportunity to prepare for the death, and had been given false reassurance. She wished that she had been told the truth at the time. Anthony and Will told similar stories:

Anthony was 14 years old when his father was involved in a road traffic accident and admitted into hospital as an emergency. Anthony was told by relatives that his father had sustained only minor injuries, when in fact these were substantial and he died that same evening.

Will was 15 at the time of his mother's death, and has never found out how his mother died or who was with her at the time in hospital. He was not allowed to go to either the chapel of rest or the funeral. With hindsight he thought that this may have been because he could have found out the details at the funeral and the family thought that it would be all too much for him.

The motives of the adults providing the Iceberg volunteers with incorrect positive news were with the best of intent and to reassure the children. This information was not at all helpful to the children, and did not give them the chance to prepare for the worst. Both Anthony and Lisa expressed the view that they would have rather been given realistic rather than over-optimistic information. In the case of both Thomas and Judith, adults other than their parents were put in the unenviable position of having to break bad news to the children. Some volunteers found out the truth about the circumstances of their parent's death only many years later, and after seeking help:

Pat was 11 years old at the time of her father's death. The events surrounding her father's death were apparently kept from her by her mother and family at the time; they were certainly not openly discussed. Pat described finding out the full details surrounding the death of her father only several years after the event, with the help and support of psychotherapy. Pat described living in an imaginary world of fantasy having no connection to the reality of the death or to her family, until she received help. Pat's family had the motive of protecting her from the pain of the death, but she said that she had been prevented from working through the issues surrounding the death of her father through this 'veil of secrecy'.

The results suggest that, in terms of understanding what is happening, the experience of death tends to be different for many children, compared with the adult experience. There were also age-related differences. Over three-quarters of the eldest age group said that they understood what was happening at the time of their parent's death. None of the pre-school group said that they had an understanding of what was happening at the time of the death.

This was an unsurprising relationship between the age of the Iceberg volunteers at the time of their parent's death and their understanding of the events. The older the children, the more they tended to understand about what was happening at the time. None of the pre-schooler group understood what was happening at the time of the death, compared to 13 per cent of those who were infants at the time of the death, and 33 per cent of the junior school volunteers. Nearly 75 per cent of the younger secondary aged volunteers reported understanding what was happening, as did 80 per cent of the older ones. For the younger children, grasping the implications of what had happened seemed to be difficult:

Amy, who was 5 years old at the time of her father's death, expressed the view that her powers of reasoning were not sufficiently developed at the time of the death for her to question the finality of death, and that this realisation came only at a much later date. It seemed perhaps unlikely that Amy would have fully absorbed the news, no matter how carefully it was explained.

Even some of the older volunteers did find that information was an issue:

> Laura was a teenager at the time of the death of her father and reported being given quite confusing information at the hospital by the nursing staff. This misled her as to the prospects of her father's survival; the hospital staff were far too optimistic and not realistic enough.

> Richard was 9 years old at the time of his father's death and described how he was totally confused by events, being in a room of hysterical women. The adults seemed not to know what to do, and Richard was left wondering what it all meant and what would happen next.

There were two issues flowing from this part of the research:

- what information is given to children about what is happening
- what the children understood about the death.

Many volunteers, especially those in the younger age groups, lacked information as to what was happening at the time of the death. The adults around these children acted as gatekeepers to information and provided only such information to the children as they, the adults, thought appropriate. It is much easier for adults to gain information at a time of crisis than it is for children, such as details of what has happened. Adults know where and how to gain information through sources such as medical staff and police. Children may be unaware of these potential routes of information, or else denied access by other adults. Information may be provided only at the discretion of the adults and then it may well be censured. Children may not also know the right or appropriate questions to ask or even what information is potentially available to them.

In the difficult circumstances after a death, it is perhaps not surprising that the needs of the children may be overlooked.

Children are generally helped by access to details of what is happening. Several volunteers were given quite false reassurances by well-meaning adults, for example after road traffic accidents or hospital admission after heart attacks. Although some volunteers did have a general understanding of what was happening at the time of the death, they still lacked precise information. Adults may underestimate children's understanding of death (Leckley 1991). If the adults around the children assume that they do not have a conceptual understanding of death, then they may well exclude them from the post death rites, with the potential of further compounding the difficulties for the children.

The pattern presented by the results from Iceberg do seem to be in line with what would intuitively be expected as regards the children's understanding of events at the time. The volunteers in the younger age groups often reported being 'protected' by their family, and were not told the full details surrounding the death of their parent. Some of the younger volunteers were not even made aware that their parent had actually been admitted to hospital or of the true nature of the seriousness of the illness, and were under the impression that their parent would soon be out of hospital. The remaining parent may not want to raise the anxiety levels of their children unduly, but this may be quite a short-term strategy. The surviving parent themselves may also have been so involved and concerned with the unfolding events, that keeping the children informed about what was happening was not a high priority. One must sympathise with either family or friends who are looking after children on behalf of the parent. In these circumstances, the carer may be very reluctant to tell the children the bad news, perceiving that this is the role of the parent. Many of the volunteers did receive the news of the death of their parent from temporary carers, rather than directly from the surviving parent.

Adults may also assume a level of knowledge that is not actually possessed by the child. By virtue of their lack of maturity and experience, children do need to have things explained to them in terms they can understand. The causes of death need to be put into appropriate language, avoiding the use of highly technical medical terminology. Many volunteers were left in the dark about their parent's death, as were some in relation to the rites surrounding the death. At times the volunteers seemed shut out of the adult world and left feeling quite isolated:

> Emily, who was aged 9 at the time of her father's death, said that her experience of the events surrounding the death was a blur, and she described that the experience was like being under water. She also said how no one ever spoke of her father or his death for many years after the event, and that it was as if he had never existed.

The adults in Emily's wider family may well have spoken about the death among themselves, but the young girl herself felt quite isolated at the time. There were other instances of families never ever speaking about the dead parent again, and even of the event of the death being so traumatic as to cause siblings to stop communicating with each other.

Some volunteers had been alerted to the potential imminent death of their parent and did have some advance warning. The anticipation of an event such as a death cannot fully prepare an individual for what is to happen, especially for children, who may not realise the full implications or the effect the news will have on them. However, some honest information of what is happening and time to prepare would seem to be a preferable option to being openly misled, however good the motives.

Chapter 11

The chapel of rest and the funeral

Introduction

One particular problem for the surviving parent is whether to involve the children in the rituals after the death, such as the chapel of rest and the funeral. The decision needs to be taken quickly, at a time of crisis within the home. The results from Iceberg show that most children will benefit from attending, although they do need careful preparation in terms of what to expect. Most of the Iceberg volunteers who were not allowed to attend these rituals felt regret, and again they had been disenfranchised of choice and excluded. This exclusion at the time of their parent's death then seemed to become an issue in itself and led to many volunteers feeling isolated as well as excluded from the family.

Depending on religion and culture, the body of the dead person may be quickly buried or else held within the family or at a chapel of rest for a short period. The Iceberg volunteers were asked whether they had visited their parent at the chapel of rest and whether they attended the funeral.

Visiting their parent at the chapel of rest

- One-fifth of the Iceberg volunteers visited their parent at the chapel of rest.

- Nearly one-third of the volunteers were forbidden to visit the chapel of rest.
- One in fourteen of the volunteers were distracted from visiting the chapel of rest.

The chapel of rest

Attending the chapel of rest and viewing the body of the deceased is a private ritual may well help the bereaved in moving from the initial shock of the death towards helping them to come to terms with what has happened. Those bereaved are then able to say their farewells to the deceased in a private setting. The surviving parent has little time after the death to decide whether or not the children should visit the chapel of rest. Making a visit to a chapel of rest involves viewing the body of a loved one, and this may be the first time that the children have actually seen a corpse.

> Annie was a young teenager at the time of her mother's death and said how she thought that seeing the body was probably a good thing, in that it convinces you that you won't see the person again.

> Ralph was 8 at the time of his mother's death and asked if he could see the body, but was refused. Ralph was also told by his father that there was no funeral, and he felt that this, and not seeing the body, left him in the state of not really believing that his mum had died.

One-fifth of the Iceberg volunteers saw their parent in the chapel of rest; the median age was the younger secondary school group. None of the volunteers in the two younger age groups visited their parent in the chapel of rest, nor did any of the oldest age group. One-fifth of the junior aged children and one-third of the younger secondary aged children visited the chapel of rest. There were no sex differences as to whether male or female volunteers visited the chapel of rest. Twice as many mums were visited as dads, over one in three compared to fewer than one in six. There seems to be no obvious explanation for this difference between the visiting of mums and dads. It may be connected to the greater proportion of fathers dying in accidents and perhaps being disfigured. Perhaps the mothers were more protective towards their children, or the fathers gave more encouragement or permission for their children to visit the chapel of rest, than did the mothers. The female Iceberg volunteers were marginally more likely to view their mother's body (55%) than they were to view their father's (45%). The reverse was the case for the male volunteers, although they were far more likely to visit their father's body (80%) than their mother's (20%). Although one-fifth of the Iceberg volunteers actually visited the chapel of rest, nearly one-third were explicitly forbidden to visit by the surviving parent. One in fourteen of the volunteers, all in the younger three age groups, reported that they were distracted at the time, so missing the opportunity of visiting the body of their parent. The distractions took various forms, including that they were not told that they had the option to see the body. Some of the volunteers were made aware of the possibility of them having been able to view the body of their parent only after it was too late; for others this was some time after the event. The realisation that they have been denied the possibility of seeing their parent in the chapel of rest may itself raise difficulties for the children later.

The volunteers were asked about how they felt about visiting the chapel of rest. About 14 per cent of the volunteers (all females) felt regret after visiting the chapel of rest, while 43 per cent of those Iceberg volunteers who viewed their parent's body in the chapel of rest reported that they had either no feelings or just felt empty after the visit, a relatively neutral response. Over one-third (36%) of the volunteers were quite positive after the visit, although 7 per cent said that they did so only as a 'matter of duty'. Thus over three-quarters of the volunteers who viewed their parent at the chapel of rest reported that it was not a negative experience.

It is impossible to say what the impact of not viewing the body would have been in those who did visit the chapel of rest. However, some knowledge was gained by asking those who did not visit the chapel of rest to report on their feelings about their non-attendance. One-third of the Iceberg volunteers who did not visit the chapel of rest reported having feelings of regret and a further one-fifth specifically felt that they had been excluded from the proceedings after the death of their parent. About 5 per cent of the volunteers reported feeling quite angry about being excluded from the events at the time. Not all the volunteers had such definite views: 14 per cent said that they were unsure about how they felt by not visiting the chapel and 5 per cent of them actually chose not to attend. Another 5 per cent of the volunteers reported that they were 'not bothered' about not visiting the chapel of rest, with 7 per cent having only vague childhood memories.

In summary, only 14 per cent of those volunteers who visited their parent at the chapel of rest expressed regret. In contrast, of those volunteers who did not attend the chapel of rest, 70 per cent felt some form of regret at not having done so, relating to issues such as exclusion from events after the death and not being allowed to say goodbye to their parent.

A surviving parent faced with having to decide whether or not to take their child to see their dead parent in the chapel of rest is in an unenviable position. There are some clues from Iceberg that may help a parent to decide.

- None of the male volunteers had any regrets after visiting the chapel of rest.

- A minority of female volunteers did have regrets after visiting the chapel of rest.

- The majority of those who did not visit the chapel expressed regrets, except when they had chosen not to visit.

Sometimes the bereaved chose not to see the dead person, preferring to retain memories of how they were in life. Others seem to gain comfort from seeing the person at rest, perhaps after a long illness, or saying their goodbyes.

Perhaps the golden rule is to allow children themselves to choose whether or not to visit their dead parent in the chapel of rest. This empowers the youngsters; some, given the choice, may actually choose not to visit the chapel of rest. The option of forbidding, distracting or misleading a child, although perhaps tempting to an adult wishing to protect children, is really only a short-term measure, and may lead to youngsters having long-term regrets. It may destroy the trust the child has in the surviving parent, potentially affecting the parent–child relationship, as well as leading to children feeling left out of things. Children will need adequate preparation for viewing their parent, especially if the body has been disfigured in an accident, although there are now very good techniques for making a body presentable.

Attending their parent's funeral

- Nearly half of the Iceberg volunteers attended their parent's funeral.

- Nearly one-quarter of the volunteers were forbidden to attend their parent's funeral.

- Over one-tenth of the volunteers were distracted from attending their parent's funeral.

The funeral

The funeral is a public event which usually follows shortly after a death, the precise timing dependent on religion, culture, family wishes and occasionally legal implications such as the holding of a post mortem or inquest. Whatever the general arrangements, the funeral is likely to be held at a time when the family has not recovered from the initial shock of the death. The surviving parent has to decide, at this difficult time, whether their children should attend the funeral of their parent. The funeral is a public rite in contrast to the chapel of rest, which is a more private and family affair.

Almost half of the Iceberg volunteers attended the funeral of their parent, more than twice the number who visited the chapel of rest. The higher number of volunteers attending the funeral is perhaps not a surprise, as generally in the UK the coffin is closed, and the perhaps perceived trauma of seeing a corpse is therefore not present. The funeral is also seen as a public event to say goodbye to the deceased, so it is perhaps more acceptable and expected that children do take part in the service.

There were no significant sex differences in those volunteers attending the funeral, as just 1 per cent more of the males attended than did females. While 40 per cent of maternal funerals were attended, nearly 50 per cent of paternal funerals were attended.

In contrast, a higher percentage of mothers were visited at the chapel of rest than were fathers. None of the volunteers in the two youngest age groups attended the funeral of their parent, and the frequency of volunteers attending increased with age. Just under half of the junior aged children and two-thirds of the younger secondary aged youngsters attended the funeral of their parent. All the volunteers who were in the oldest age group attended the funeral.

- None of the Iceberg volunteers attending the funeral reported a negative or detrimental effect.

- Two-thirds of the volunteers attending the funeral said that doing so was a positive or helpful event.

- None of the volunteers reported being frightened by the experience of attending the funeral or regretted having attended.

One in eight of the Iceberg volunteers said that they felt nothing when attending the funeral. Others reported that attending the funeral was a positive event, and some felt that it had helped their grieving and let them say goodbye to their parent. One reported laughing on hearing somebody singing out of tune at the ceremony. Cindy, Diana and Samantha had all attended their fathers' funerals:

Cindy was a teenager at the time of the death of her father and related that attending the funeral was a 'good experience' for her. Cindy felt supported by the large number of people who also attended the funeral, and that it provided her with the opportunity to both say goodbye, as well as to see how well her father had been regarded by others.

Diana said that she would have been 'detached from reality and felt excluded' if she had not attended her dad's funeral. Attending the funeral was of particular importance in terms of Diana both accepting the reality and also feeling part of the family at that difficult time for them all.

Samantha felt that attending the funeral and seeing the coffin did help to bring the reality of her dad's death home to her, and helped in the grieving process. Seeing the coffin was proof that her dad would not be returning.

In contrast with some of those visiting the chapel of rest, none of the volunteers attending the funeral reported having a negative or bad experience. Perhaps some volunteers reporting feeling nothing at the funeral were still in shock after the death of their parent, and attending it could well have helped them to grasp the reality of what had happened, as related by Diana. It is, of course, impossible to say what the impact of not attending the funeral would have been on those who did attend. However, some guide can be gained by the answers of those volunteers who did not attend, about their feelings about their non-attendance at their parent's funeral.

- Over half of the Iceberg volunteers had not attended their parent's funeral, and a large proportion of this group felt that this had caused them difficulty later in their life.

- Over three-quarters of those volunteers who did not go to the funeral of their parent wished that they had so attended.

Over one-third of those not attending the funeral had strong feelings of regret, over half of them feeling that they had been excluded from family events at the time of the death of their parent. Other feelings expressed by some volunteers included anger, hurt, frustration and that they had not been allowed to grieve effectively for their dead parent.

Around one-fifth of the volunteers were unsure, not bothered or felt nothing about not attending the funeral. There were sex differences: two-fifths of the female volunteers expressed feelings of regret about not attending the funeral, compared to one-quarter of the male volunteers. More of the male volunteers were excluded from the funeral, although they also had a lower rate of reported regret. Only male volunteers perceived that their family had 'protected them' by shielding them from attending the funeral.

Such 'protection' runs fundamentally counter to the ideas of being truthful with children, and including them in the proceedings after a death, to help them with their own grieving (LeShan 1979; Raphael 1984). Such a strategy is likely to be successful only in the short term, as the youngsters will sooner or later either realise or be told that they could have attended the funeral, with the potential later for anger and regret. Fewer of the Iceberg volunteers were actually forbidden to attend the funeral than to go to the chapel of rest, although more were actually distracted from attending the funeral. The most common distractions were to send the children to school or to a friend's house for the day. Over one-third (36%) of the volunteers were forbidden or distracted from visiting the chapel of rest, and 35 per cent of them were forbidden or distracted from attending the funeral.

> Sheena, who was 8 at the time of her father's death, recalled how she watched a cortège passing by the school playground, only realising later it was her father's cortège on its way to the funeral. Sheena had been sent to school and was totally unaware that it was the day of her father's funeral; it was only by chance that as the cortège passed by she was out at play in the playground of her school.

Sometimes children may need positive adult encouragement to think carefully about attending the funeral, as they may realise what they have missed only many years later:

> Tony was a junior aged child at the time of the death of his father. He did not attend the funeral, although he had no strong views at the time, and was not really 'bothered'. It was only fourteen years later, after the death of another close relative, that he then began to have pangs of regret as to not having attended the funeral of his father, and not having taken the chance for a last goodbye.

Final thoughts on children attending the funeral and chapel of rest

Few volunteers visited the chapel of rest to see their parent, although nearly half of them did attend their parent's funeral. In my experience of working with bereaved adults, parents agonise as to whether or not to allow their children to visit their parent at the chapel of rest or to attend the funeral. It is received wisdom that counsellors generally consider that attending both the chapel of rest and the funeral is helpful for the bereaved. Since these rites are thought to be beneficial for bereaved adults, it also seems reasonable to consider that they may be helpful to bereaved children. Freda was one of the mothers who took part in Iceberg:

> Freda thought that it was important for both her children, one a teenager and the other a young primary child, to go to both the chapel of rest and the funeral, to provide a proper 'ending' for the children in relation to their father.

> Melanie was 15 years old at the time of her father's death and was not allowed to go to either the chapel of rest or the funeral. Melanie said how she felt that she was left 'on the side' and out of things.

Melanie's view was that parents really need advice regarding children being involved in the rituals after the death. She also thought that children should be actively encouraged to visit the chapel of rest and attend the funeral, unless they really had 'violent' objections. Children do need to be prepared if they are to become involved in these rights, especially if it is the first time they have experienced the event. The family is likely still to be in a state of shock after the death. Children may well be left out of proceedings at this time, perhaps because it is considered that they have no place or do not need to be so involved, or because the adults are simply too focused on their own grief to consider that of the children.

> Shelly was a teenager at the time of her father's death and was not allowed to attend either the chapel of rest or the funeral. Shelly described how she felt 'surplus to requirements' at the time, but felt that she had not really said goodbye to her father, something she has much regretted.

Children may need the active support of adults to become involved in these post death rituals. The results of Iceberg do seem to support the notion that it is generally a good idea for the children to attend the funeral of their parent, although there are no data regarding the younger age groups. None of the Iceberg volunteers attending the funeral reported having any negative effects; the majority felt that it had been a positive event. Of those volunteers not attending the funeral, three-quarters wished, with hindsight, that they had taken part. It seems that there is nothing to lose, but much to gain, by children attending the funeral. Children may well benefit from attending the funeral of their parents, as part of their grieving process (Duffy 1995). It could be contended that the grieving process may be inhibited if children are not allowed to attend their parent's funeral, and an environment of denial could be created (Goldman 1994).

The position regarding the chapel of rest is not quite so clear for girls. There were both positive and negative reports by the volunteers who visited their parent at the chapel of rest, as well as regrets by some of those who had not. Perhaps the golden rule is to ask children and allow them if they so wish to attend either of these rites, but then not to force those who do not want to attend. It is also very important to prepare the children for the experiences of viewing a dead body and attending the funeral. Telling children what to expect at both events should help; for example, they need to be told that the coffin will move behind curtains at a crematorium. Helping children in this way will reduce the likelihood of them having fantasies about what will occur.

The overall message from Iceberg in relation to both the chapel of rest and the funeral is that young people benefit from being given the choice as to whether or not to attend these rituals. None of the volunteers attending the funeral reported any adverse effects. In contrast, many of them who were not allowed to attend the funeral reported long-term difficulties such as feeling regret, anger and having been excluded from family involvement. If children are not involved in these rites, then not only are they unable to say goodbye to the deceased, but they may also feel isolated and excluded from the family proceedings. The latter, at a time of family crisis, may have as much impact as the former.

Chapter 12

The return to school

The time the Iceberg volunteers had off school after the death

The Iceberg volunteers were asked how long they had off school after the death of their parent.

- Nearly half (44%) of the Iceberg volunteers went straight back to school immediately after the death of their parent, without having any break at all.

- One-fifth of the parental deaths occurred in the school holidays, so that an immediate return to school was not possible.

- One-sixth of the volunteers remained off school for a week after the death of their parent.

There were minor sex differences, in that 50 per cent of the female volunteers and 40 per cent of the male volunteers returned straight back to school after the death. There was no clear indication of what the volunteers were doing at home during this period of time. One-sixth of the Iceberg volunteers returned to school a week after the death. One in fourteen of the volunteers returned to school after just having two or three days at home, and one in twenty of the volunteers were off school for several weeks.

How long children should stay off school after the death of their parent is another difficult question for the remaining parent. The parent may think that the sooner the children return to school the better, in terms of them achieving some form of normality. There is evidence that some volunteers thought that their school provided them with such normality, and for these their returning to school was not problematic. This 'normality' was merely a return to their routine and to their peers, and was not to a planned reception or transition by the school. For some of the Iceberg volunteers this lack of interaction and attention by their school was welcomed and may have related to the contrast with the grieving parent and the sad memories at home.

> Simon was a teenager at the time of the death of his father, and he felt that it was quite a relief to get away from the oppressive atmosphere at home, and that the return to school was quite a positive event for him.

Many others reported that they were isolated and felt ignored within the school system. The normality reported seemed to be an unplanned response to the volunteers, the school simply leaving them alone, which a minority found helpful. It seems quite ironic that some schools actually seemed to help the volunteers by doing nothing!

Some volunteers had reported feelings of being excluded at home by not taking part in the chapel of rest and funeral. Children may feel further excluded if they return to school very quickly and they may perhaps benefit from a brief period at home. The issues and motives around why the volunteers were kept off school are unclear. This may have related to the needs of the surviving parent for company, or for help with housework or looking after younger children. Several volunteers, including some of the males, told how they were now suddenly expected to take a greater responsibility around the home. Children may have been involved in just being with their parent and interacting with relations and friends, or helping with the arrangements. They could be included in the arrangements after the death, providing ideas for the funeral service, such as hymns. The home may be quite a centre of activity at this time shortly after the death of the parent, and it may be helpful for the children to be involved rather than perhaps feeling left out by being at school. Friends and other members of the family may well visit the home at this time to pay their respects.

All of the Iceberg volunteers who were of infant age returned to school immediately after the death, as did half of the other volunteers. There were no other interactions between the time off school and either the age or the sex of the volunteers.

How the Iceberg volunteers felt on returning to their school after the death

The death of the parent would have impacted highly on the home environment and also on the immediate social and relationships circle. This may not be the case at school and the death may not even have been common knowledge, unless it took place in particularly traumatic or tragic circumstances. Most volunteers had returned quickly to school after the death.

- One-quarter of the Iceberg volunteers felt that they were ignored on returning to their school.

- One-fifth of the volunteers felt that they were isolated on returning to their school.

- One-eighth of the volunteers said that they felt normal on returning to their school.

- One in six of the volunteers felt embarrassed on returning to their school.

The majority of the Iceberg volunteers found that returning to their school was not a positive experience for them. When they were asked to describe their feelings on when returning to their school, most reported just one predominating feeling.

Laurie was 13 at the time of the death of her father, and she said how she felt that she was ignored; it was as if she had done something to be ashamed of somehow.

Sean was at infant school at the time of his father's death and felt that school stereotyped him as being from a 'single family', as if there was some fault attached. Sean did not feel at all comfortable with the response of the school to the death.

Terry was at primary school when his father had died, and reflected that he thought that his school had done nothing, because they were not aware of the possibilities and potential difficulties flowing from the death.

Schools seem to have had no procedures for the receiving and transition of the volunteers back into school, or the teachers generally may have found it difficult and not know how to respond to the youngsters. In any event, the reality for the volunteers was that they felt ignored on their return. Feeling ignored was reported across all the age groups except by the pre-schoolers. These young children may simply not have been fully aware at the time, or perhaps they may have forgotten the events at the time. One-third of the volunteers who experienced the death of their mother reported feeling ignored, compared with one-fifth who had experienced a paternal death. The difference is interesting, although there seems to be no obvious explanation. It may relate in part to their home situation, in that if their mother had been the main carer, they now lacked attention at home and perhaps this feeling of lack of attention transferred back into their feelings on returning to their school. The volunteers would, in any event, have had a reduction in parental attention, with half the parenting team gone and the other half grieving. It may be that the volunteers whose fathers had died were given more attention than those whose mothers had died.

One-fifth of the Iceberg volunteers felt quite isolated on their return to school. This was reported in one-seventh of maternal deaths and one-quarter of paternal deaths, a reverse of the sex difference for volunteers feeling ignored.

In summary, nearly half of the Iceberg volunteers felt either isolated or ignored when they returned to school after the death of their parent. In contrast, one-sixth felt embarrassed on returning to their school, and these volunteers did not welcome receiving any attention at school. There were no sex differences between either the volunteers or the parent dying, and those reporting embarrassment.

> Jane described feeling like she was in a glass bubble on her return to her school, this being a vivid and visual impression of her feelings of embarrassment at the time of the death. Jane was anxious to avoid receiving any attention at all from teachers in connection with the death of her parent.

One-eighth of the Iceberg volunteers described feeling quite 'normal' on returning to their school. This was reported by one-fifth of the males and just over one-tenth of the females. Just over one-tenth of the volunteers had no recall of the events at the time of their return to school, and these were all in the lowest three age groups, with marginally more reports by the males. About 6 per cent of the Iceberg volunteers were uncertain about their feelings and another 4 per cent said that they just felt different from the other children, but that it was difficult to describe in what way. Other feelings included those of feeling relief, fragile and stupid. Relief related to the ability of the Iceberg volunteers to return to normality at their schools, and that at least in some ways, life had not changed. The feeling of fragility expressed by some volunteers is self-explanatory and creates quite a visual image. The feeling of stupidity was also allied to that of some volunteers feeling embarrassed and different from the other children at their school.

The perception by the majority of the Iceberg volunteers was that their schools generally did not respond well to them on their return. They may well have brought 'baggage' of emotions with them from home to their school, and these may have been expressed through non-verbal communication, or through a reluctance to talk with others at school. Ultimately these negative signals from the volunteers may well have affected their later interactions with their peers and teachers, who may have thought that the volunteers just wanted to be left alone.

School could potentially play quite a positive role with these children. Teachers are adults, and could be expected to take the initiative at a time of crisis. They could perhaps use a gentle approach, making bereaved children aware that there was support available if it was needed, although not pushing the children, who may actually not welcome such an interaction. It may be that teachers do not want to move from their position of a professional teaching relationship to one of a more personal relationship (Abrams 1993). For some of these teachers, interacting with bereaved children is perhaps an 'emotional bridge too far', although there may be great benefits for the children by those teachers who do cross that bridge, and make the first approach.

How their school helped the Iceberg volunteers on their return

It would seem reasonable to assume a connection between how well their school helped the volunteers on their return, and their feelings on their return. It must be remembered that the perceptions are those of the volunteers when they were children and are their reality, even if this was not as intended by the teachers. Most of the Iceberg volunteers did not have positive feelings on returning to their school. It is impossible to partial out whether the feelings of the volunteers related to their feelings around the death of their parent, or if it related to their reception at school; it was probably a combination of both.

The volunteers were asked how their schools helped them on their return:

- Two thirds of the Iceberg volunteers said that their schools did nothing on their return after the death of their parent.

- One-tenth of the volunteers said that just one teacher spoke to them, which they regarded as a positive action.

- One-tenth of the volunteers said that teachers had primed their peers, and that they regarded this as a positive response.

Philip was a teenager at the time of his father's death. Philip described his return to school being as if the death had not happened, as there was no response at all from anybody at his school.

The reports made by Philip and other volunteers are their perceptions, which does not of course mean that the school actually did nothing. However, this was the reality for the volunteers, and for any help to be effective, it needs to be so perceived by those being helped. There was a sex difference, as 71 per cent of the female volunteers thought that their school had done nothing, compared with 60 per cent of the males. The females may have had higher expectations of their schools in terms of helping, or they have had greater needs than did the males.

Only 4 per cent of volunteers had no recall of the events at the time, suggesting that overall the return of the volunteers to their schools had made quite an impact. A similar number of volunteers thought that their school helped as it provided them with 'normality'.

> Marjorie was a teenager at the time of her father's death and she said that she was helped by her school just being 'normal' and by immersing herself in her work.

Just over one-tenth of the Iceberg volunteers said that one teacher had spoken to them about the death, and this was a significant event they regarded as helpful: about 16 per cent of males and 9 per cent of females reported this. The importance for the volunteers, at the time after their parent's death, seemed to be that this was regarded as an act of acknowledgement of their loss. One-tenth of the volunteers related how the teachers at school had 'briefed' their peers, and had alerted these other children in their class or school about the death of their parent. This was also perceived as being a very positive action by some volunteers at that time. It seemed to help by removing a large degree of uncertainty for the volunteers, in that they did not have to wonder about who at school knew about the death, and also relieved them of the task of telling others. The volunteers may have been unaware that a briefing had taken place and the school's responses may be underreported in Iceberg. Some children may not have welcomed such a public recognition of the death of their parent, and it would always be prudent for schools to liaise with the family and youngster and to act with caution before making a public announcement about the death. Some of the responses by schools to the volunteers were not always helpful:

Peter was 6 years old at the time of the death of his father and said that he was allowed to stay inside his classroom at school during break-times, this being the only response of the school to his parent's death. It was some recognition, but did not really seem to be an appropriate response. Peter's view was not sought on the matter and he actually felt even more excluded and isolated by this action.

Another volunteer said that she was 'let off' homework for a short time after the death. Other volunteers reported receiving very insensitive treatment at their schools:

Toni was a teenager at the time of her father's sudden death, and was actually ridiculed by one of her teachers, as she was unable to read out loud in front of her class without stuttering and stammering. Toni connected these difficulties with the death of her father, and said that she was made to feel very 'silly' by this particular teacher.

This seems to have been a very insensitive approach to the girl. It is hard to believe that the teacher did not know about the death of Toni's father, but if this was the case then it reflected badly on the school's system of communication. Another possibility is that the teacher was unable to make the connection between the death and the difficulties, or did not think that the death would have any impact on the teenager. Other volunteers told how teachers had criticised the standard of their work shortly after the death, and they found this quite distressing at the time. Keith had difficulties with his peer group when he returned to school:

Keith said he had been teased about the death of his father, this leading to fights, in which he was both blamed and punished. Keith told how he thought that it was very unfair that he was punished, especially as he felt that a large part of his world had collapsed after the death of his father.

In contrast, two other volunteers, both girls, thought that their teachers became more tolerant towards them after the deaths of their parents. This may have reflected the intentions of their teachers, or just been the girls' own perceptions. Other volunteers felt that other adults were also more kindly towards them, such as buying them treats or taking them out with their own children. The reason for these favours, which was assumed to be the death of their parent, was never raised or discussed.

Most volunteers thought that their school had actually done nothing to help them on their return after the death of their parent, some were helped by the teachers at their school either listening to them, or else priming their peers about the death. In contrast, some volunteers reported that this apparent inaction by their school was positive. The reason for this is that the inaction by their schools, and carrying on as usual, gave some degree of normality, although this does not seem to have been a planned and considered intervention by their schools!

The Iceberg volunteers were asked to score their schools in relation to the help that they had received over the period of the bereavement. The volunteers were asked to score their schools on a scale from 0 to 10. A zero score indicated that the school had been no help during the bereavement and 10 was the highest score that could be allocated. Table 12.1 shows the scores given to their school by the Iceberg volunteers.

Well over half (57%) of the Iceberg volunteers rated their schools at zero, in terms of the help they perceived they received during the period of bereavement. This was the lowest score that could be given and reflected the large proportion of volunteers who considered that their school provided them with no effective help after the death of their parent. The average score given by the volunteers to their schools was 1.8. Only 14 per cent of the volunteers rated the help given to them by their schools as being between 6 and 10.

Table 12.1 The volunteers' rating of how they felt school helped during the period of bereavement	
Score	%
0	57
1	7
2	9
3	9
4	4
5	0
6	6
7	1
8	0
9	6
10	1

There was a difference between the sexes, as the male volunteers gave their schools a higher average rating of 2.7, compared to the female volunteer average score of 1.4 (Table 12.2). The males perceived that their schools helped them more than did the females. There was also a weak pattern suggesting that the older the volunteers were when they were bereaved, then the higher they rated their school in terms of helping. The overall scores were quite low, but tie in with other reports from the volunteers, that they actually received little direct help from their schools. The scores of the volunteers were then compared with scores given by those mothers who also took part in the survey.

	Female children		Male children		Mothers	
Table 12.2 The volunteers' rating of how they felt school helped: females, males and mothers						
	Mean	Range	Mean	Range	Mean	Range
Total	1.4	0–10	2.7	0–10	6.3	0–10

The mothers of the bereaved children rated the help given to their children by their schools as a mean of 6.3, over three times the mean score of the children. The perceptions of the Iceberg mothers and children differ, and it seems that parents may well overestimate the help that their children are actually receiving from their school after the death. This does perhaps hint that the schools were attempting more than the Iceberg volunteers realised, but that it was not as effective as perceived by the mothers as a group. This was not the view of all the mothers:

> Tanya told how the schools her children attended were unsupportive: they chose to ignore the death and offered no support or special consideration to the family.

Schools and teachers could potentially play a supportive role at the time of stress for bereaved children, although clearly this did not seem to be generally happening for the volunteers (Sharp and Cowie 1998). Children may find school a refuge after a parental death or separation, although teachers have been perceived as being more sympathetic to pupils affected by parental separation rather than by parental death (Lewis 1992). For a large proportion of the Iceberg volunteers, school was not a safe haven from a grieving home and provided them with little support, although a minority of the volunteers found that their return to school provided them with normality, and as such this was helpful.

Did their schools help to prepare the Iceberg volunteers for the bereavement?

The volunteers were asked about their perceptions of how school had helped them at the time after the death of their parent. Although the focus of Iceberg was on the volunteers' experience when they were at school, these could not be taken out of the context of their home.

All the volunteers thought that their schools had done nothing to help to prepare them for their bereavement. This was an unambiguous response from all the volunteers. This begs two questions, one of which is whether schools should have such a role, and the other is how the schools could have better helped the volunteers.

School could potentially help to prepare children for their future life, with a focus on life skills, although this is a question of educational philosophy, and there are other priorities in the curriculum. Some teachers thought that they had a role to play in the area of loss education (Leckley 1991). Teachers will gain in confidence in supporting and interacting with bereaved children after receiving training in the area of loss (Urbanowicz 1994). Schools potentially could help children prepare for losses in life through death and loss education (Sharp and Cowie 1998). It should also be borne in mind that many children today experience the loss of a parent through parental separation (Holland 2000).

How schools could have improved their response to the Iceberg volunteers

This was one of the key questions in the Iceberg research, and was crucial in responding to the needs of bereaved children in the future. Those who took part in the project, having had the benefit of hindsight and some time of reflection, were able to make a positive contribution to helping currently bereaved children. It was hoped that these results in particular would be of interest to teachers and others involved in supporting children who have experienced loss. Evidence from much of the previous research suggested that schools rated the area of child bereavement highly, although teachers often thought that they lacked the skills to help their pupils. Schools seemed to perceive that they could have a role in supporting bereaved children, but were perhaps unsure how to help. The Iceberg volunteers were asked how their schools could have helped them more. This was intended as a trawl for ideas from the volunteers, as individuals having actually been through the experience of having a parent die when they were at school.

- Over half of the volunteers would have been helped after the death of their parent by having someone available at school to listen to them.

- One-quarter of the volunteers would have been helped by just a simple acknowledgement of the death of their parent.

- One-quarter of the volunteers said that they would have been helped at their school if they had received 'death education'.

- One-tenth of the volunteers thought that they would have been helped if their teachers had told their peers at school about the death of their parent.

Some of these results do tie in with the reports that many of the Iceberg volunteers made about feeling isolated and ignored when they returned to school, and also of them finding their teachers difficult to approach. Some volunteers were quite specific about how they could have been helped and how children could be helped in the future.

Helen described how there was no one at her secondary school who she could talk with about the death of her father. Helen felt strongly about this and suggested that a person should be allocated for this specific role in schools. She also thought that it needed to be someone who had actually been bereaved and could empathise more fully with children who were going through the experience.

Florence was also a teenager at the time of her father's death and she made similar comments, adding that it would have helped her if teachers had more of an awareness and empathy with pupils going through the experience of having had a parent die. She felt that teachers as a group were not at all sympathetic, and that they would benefit from more training and also from a greater awareness of issues in this area. Florence added that she thought that the surviving parents also needed advice on how to help their children at the time after the death.

Maggie said that she felt very bitter how, as a teenager, that no one at her school had 'bothered' to say anything at all to her about the death. There was a comment made on Maggie's end of year report that she had had a difficult year, which she thought was a remarkable understatement of how she had really felt! Maggie's teachers would likely not have intended to be so insensitive and may have been horror struck to realise how she felt about the comments.

Children could be better helped to understand death through their teachers being open with them (Mishne 1992). Teachers could also help the children through accepting and coping with their feelings after the death of a parent.

The suggestion by half of the Iceberg volunteers that their schools could have helped just by listening to them was a relatively simple way of providing support. Many volunteers thought that they would have been helped if there had been somebody just to listen to them at the time of their parent's death. This is a very low-level intervention, not counselling, simply making a basic human connection with the youngsters. Teachers may find this quite an uncomfortable role, not only because of their own potential feelings in the area of loss, but also as it steps outside the professional teacher–pupil relationship and into the 'dangerous' area of emotions. Those teachers who overcame this taboo and made a more personal connection with the volunteers did significantly help them.

Just over one-third of the Iceberg volunteers thought that counselling would have helped them at their school after the death of their parent. Counselling is a more specialist intervention than just listening, and the volunteers may actually have been helped by having the opportunity to talk things through with a teacher, perhaps removing the need for the more specialised help. The volunteers may also not have had a real understanding of counselling.

Many secondary schools in the USA and Australia have their own school counsellor or psychologist, although this is still quite rare in British schools. Educational psychologists, who provide psychological support to schools, are very thin on the ground and are not always able to provide this type of ongoing support. It may not always be appropriate for an outside agency to become involved in a school, other than on an advisory basis. The health service may also be able to provide psychiatric support to bereaved children, but this is introducing more professions, less likely to have had a background in education, and also with the possibility of the children then having a formal record of psychiatric involvement. It would perhaps be more appropriate for bereaved children to be initially talking things through with somebody they knew, such as a trusted teacher, rather than with a stranger from outside their school. If nothing else, the use of an outsider brings with it the message that death and bereavement are issues with which the school staff cannot cope. This must surely be de-skilling for teachers, who could perhaps best help bereaved pupils by gaining some basic skills in the area of loss. It may be that, if a light intervention is not having an effect, a more formal counselling approach is appropriate, but this could be something that is tried later rather than sooner after the death of a parent.

One-quarter of the Iceberg volunteers thought that their school could have helped them just by acknowledging their loss. The volunteers perceived that this simple act would have helped them at the time of the death of their parent. This does link in with the reports of many volunteers feeling isolated and ignored at school and that just some simple recognition could have helped them at the time. The volunteers often said that their teachers would avoid mentioning the death in their presence, although those few teachers who did have the courage to talk with the volunteers were very well received. Simply expressing regret that the parent had died would probably have been sufficient. In contrast, the Iceberg volunteers often tended to be faced with what was described by several as a 'blank wall' at school. The mind-set of their teachers may well have been that they did not want to cause upset by mentioning the death. The mind-set of the volunteers seemed to have been that their teachers were not interested in what for them had been a very significant life event, and therefore their conclusion was that their teachers did not care. The teachers may have been worried about what to say to the volunteers, and that any words spoken would come out in a clumsy way. This would have been unlikely to be of concern to the volunteers at the time, although the act of acknowledgement and recognition would have been a powerfully positive event for them.

One-quarter of the Iceberg volunteers thought that their school could have helped more by explaining things to them at the time. This is not death education, but rather providing them with information about what is happening at a time of crisis. Many volunteers said that they did not really understand what was happening at the time of the death of their parent. Many volunteers were quite confused and lacked information about what was happening. To play a role here, the school would need to liaise closely with the children's parent and family to determine what is happening, as well as to check out the accuracy of the circumstances, and perhaps to offer support. The school would also need to ensure that the parent was comfortable with the release of appropriate information to their own and perhaps others' children. Some families may have the view that the school has no role to play here.

One-tenth of the Iceberg volunteers said that it would have helped them if their teachers had told their peers that their parent had died, and also if all the teachers at their school had been made aware of the circumstances. The issues here seem to relate to both communication systems and policies within schools, and it is also very important that the non-teaching school staff are not forgotten. It would also be prudent to liaise with the family before making an announcement to others at school, to ensure the accuracy of the information and also that the family is comfortable with its release, although it may be common knowledge in the neighbourhood.

There were other responses from the volunteers providing suggestions as to how school could have better helped them after the death of their parent. These included providing reassurance to the children and being more open and honest with them. It may not always be possible for teachers to give reassurances in some circumstances, and it would be quite wrong for them so to do unless they themselves have accurate information. Having a good relationship between the school and the family is always important, especially in the sensitive area of death, but ultimately a good relationship will bring benefits for the children. These suggestions are perhaps also reflections of the isolation that was felt by many volunteers at the time of the death.

Other volunteers suggested that being involved with group sessions within their school would have helped them at the time of the death. This would have enabled the volunteers to gain access to and harness peer support, the idea being to involve other youngsters who had gone through the same experience of having a parent die.

A small minority of the Iceberg volunteers wished that their school had more explicitly enabled them to share and work through their feelings. These volunteers would have welcomed a more active facilitation of their grief. One-quarter of the volunteers thought that it would have helped them if loss or death education had been included in the taught curriculum at their school. One-third of the females thought that death or loss education would have helped them in connection with the death of their parent.

In comparison one-sixth of the males held that view. There was a marked difference between the sexes, which could have been a reflection of the greater perceived need of the female volunteers. Some of the female volunteers suggested that it would have helped them if 'life skills' classes, including loss and death education, had been available at their school, and yet others thought that their teachers generally needed more training in the area of death and loss.

There was a variety of strategies that the Iceberg volunteers felt would have helped them at the time of the death of their parent and within the context of their school. Half would have been helped at their school simply by having a teacher to listen to them after the death of their parent and one-quarter of them would have been helped by some simple acknowledgement of their loss at school.

Neither of the above strategies seems to be very onerous in terms of resources, and they do seem to be relatively simple procedures. These strategies are simply the school staff making human links with the bereaved children. Some of the other suggestions made by the Iceberg volunteers are more expensive in terms of resources: the employment of school counsellors has implications in terms of costs. Death education would involve curriculum development and changes.

Schools are potentially well placed to support bereaved children, and this was a view shared by many volunteers. However, adequate training is needed to enable teachers to become more confident in the area of death and loss (Rowling 1994; Urbanowicz 1994). A few volunteers were adamant that their school could have done absolutely nothing to have helped them after the death of their parent, such was the impact of the event on their lives.

> Colin was at primary school when his father had died, and the school did not respond at all. Colin's view was that really there was nothing that his school could actually have done, they could not have replaced his father.

Did the Iceberg volunteers have any death or loss education at their school?

The volunteers were asked whether they actually had any loss or death education at their school. Only one volunteer had any loss or death education. My previous research in Humberside (Holland 1993; Holland and Ludford 1995) found that there was little loss education taking place in schools. My later research, which included secondary schools in the Humberside, Sunderland and Newcastle areas, was more optimistic (Holland 2000). In some secondary schools, loss education was in place, led by enthusiastic teachers who regarded the area to be very important. There was little reporting of liaison between schools and individual teachers, although clearly some excellent work was in progress.

Did schools help or hinder the Iceberg volunteers with their bereavement?

The volunteers were asked whether they thought that their schools had helped or hindered with grieving after the death of their parent, and was another measure of the volunteers' perceptions about their schools:

- Nearly half (44%) of the Iceberg volunteers thought that their schools gave them no help.

- One-quarter of the volunteers thought that their school had provided them with normality.

- One-tenth of the volunteers thought that their school was 'OK'.

Most volunteers were able to remember back to this period in time and they did have a view as to whether their school either helped or hindered them. The males were generally far more positive about their schools: only one-third of them said that schools gave them no help, compared with half of the females. It could be that the schools tended to respond better to the male volunteers or that the sexes had different expectations or perceptions of their schools. The female volunteers may have expected more help relatively than did their male counterparts.

One-quarter of the Iceberg volunteers said that their school helped them by providing them with a normality that was missing from their life at home; there were no sex differences in this reporting. An irony is that their school's apparent inaction in not responding to some of the Iceberg volunteers when they were children seemed to have helped them! One-third of the volunteers reported normality two years after the death. This does partly tend to support the idea of school being a potential safe haven for children after the death of a parent (Lewis 1992).

One-tenth of the volunteers reported that on balance they were comfortable with their school and how the teachers responded. One-eighth of the volunteers said that their schools neither helped nor hindered them, but had a broadly neutral effect after the death of their parent.

Two-thirds of the Iceberg volunteers reported that their school was either broadly neutral or that it actually helped them in some way after the death of their parent.

The positive benefits of school included providing an escape from the more problematic environment of home and giving the volunteers the opportunity to be with their peers and friends.

Some found that their school life was a positive distraction from the difficulties that they were experiencing at home. Other volunteers said that individual teachers had responded to them in a kindly manner, or had listened to them, which they considered had helped them in terms of their grieving. Some volunteers reported being 'smothered' by attention at school and subsequently feeling quite embarrassed about receiving this unwanted attention.

Just under half the volunteers said that their school either was hindering or was, in some way, a negative aspect after the death of their parent. Many volunteers did not consider that their schools had actively helped them during their time of grieving, although there was a significant number for whom the school either provided normality as a positive benefit, or was at least neutral. For many the help provided by school was the possibly unplanned response of leaving them alone, and restoring what the volunteers considered was normality. There is yet again the issue of training in the area of loss, which tends to be effective in helping teachers to become more confident in this area (Urbanowicz 1994).

Did the Iceberg volunteers have more time off school?

This question related to the experiences of the volunteers in the medium term (i.e. the period following the time of their inital grieving – generally 18 months and beyond), and was to investigate whether they generally tended to have more or less time off their school after the death of their parent.

Just over half (56%) of the Iceberg volunteers said that they did not have more time off school after the death of their parent; the percentages were the same for the sex of the volunteers and of the parent dying. About 10 per cent of the volunteers said that they actually had less time off school after the death. This may perhaps have been because it was more difficult for the surviving parent to arrange for the care of the children when they were ill, so that they were now marginally more likely to send them to school when they had a minor ailment illness. There were other reasons, such as described by Jennifer:

> Jennifer told how she actually had less time off school after the death, as she did not now spend as much time at home being with her dying mother.

Just over one-quarter of the volunteers said that they did have more time off school after the death of their parent. This was for a variety of reasons, including illness, although one in ten now thought that their illnesses were psychological rather than physical in origin.

William was 10 at the time his dad had died and he told
how his mum had kept him off school for company and her
needs at the time after the death.

A small minority of the volunteers reported playing truant in
the period immediately after the death; this again was equally
spilt between the sexes. About 5 per cent of the male volunteers said that they had now become school phobic and
avoided school. There may have been a combination of factors
in play for the truants. The volunteers were perhaps now more
easily able to evade the surviving parent, especially if they
were out at work. There may now have been nobody at home,
in contrast to previous time, and in any event, the parenting
team had been halved.

If school was not seen as a refuge and the Iceberg volunteers
had reported feeling isolated and ignored at school, then they
may not have wished to engage with what they perceived as an
unfriendly system. In these circumstances, the attraction of
school could have declined to such a point that the marginal
benefits of other activities, even solitude, were more attractive
than their school. Many of their teachers may have considered
that it was inappropriate for them to become involved in supporting the volunteers, or they may even have thought that
there was not an issue around the death of the parent. Playing
truant can perhaps be seen as a logical response by some of the
Iceberg volunteers, made easier by the halving of the parental
management team, as well as the surviving parent probably
going through the process of grieving and being more
distractible. These are difficulties that arose, not because of the
death itself, but through secondary factors that flowed directly
from the death. There also seems to have been a perceived
unintended uncaring response from school, as well as less
parental management. This does contrast with the view that

teenagers may regard their school as a safe haven after the death of a parent (Lewis 1992).

Chapter 13

The isolation of the Iceberg volunteers

How isolated the Iceberg volunteers felt during the first year after the death

Towards the end of the interview, the Iceberg volunteers were asked to rate how isolated they had felt during the first year after the death of their parent. Table 13.1 shows the scores.

Table 13.1 The volunteers' rating of how isolated they felt during the first year after the death of their parent	
Rating	%
0	47
1	8
2	9
3	7
4	2
5	1
6	3
7	1
8	2
9	1
10	3

The volunteers were asked to allocate a score on a scale from zero to 10 rating how isolated they had felt during the first year after the death of their parent. The lower the reported score, the greater the feeling of isolation perceived, zero being the most isolated and 10 being the least isolated. Nearly half the volunteers gave a score of zero, and the average score was 2. There was a slight sex difference in the scores, the average male volunteer scored 2.2, compared with the average female scoring 1.9. The females therefore reported feeling marginally more isolated over this period than did the males. There was also a weak pattern suggesting that the older the volunteers were when they were bereaved, then the less isolated they had felt.

How approachable were the Iceberg volunteers' teachers after the death?

The teaching staff are arguably the most important resource possessed by schools and the volunteers' perceptions of how well their schools dealt with their return will mainly relate to how well the volunteers thought that their teachers had responded. In addition, a positive response by teachers is also a good role model for the other children at the school. Schools generally did not seem to respond well to the volunteers, nor to take the initiative. The volunteers were asked if the teachers at their school were easy to approach, if they needed to talk.

- One in ten of the Iceberg volunteers did not want to talk with teachers after the death of their parent.

- One in twenty of the volunteers did find their teachers easy to approach after the death of their parent.

Three-quarters of the Iceberg volunteers said that their teachers were not easy to approach after the death of their parent. Two thirds of the volunteers said that their school had done nothing to help them on their return after the death. Four-fifths of the females and two-thirds of the males made this report. The female volunteers had also reported a greater incidence of their schools not helping them initially on their return, which could reflect a greater female need or expectation for support. Some volunteers found that their teachers were too remote to even consider approaching them.

> Tina was of infant age at the time of her father's death, and she related how she found her teachers at school detached and formal. Tina found the response of her teachers to be very aloof, and would have made an approach to them impossible.

It may have been that Tina's teachers did not know how to respond to her after the death, or they thought that the formal approach was the most helpful to her, which was not the case. Tina may have been helped had her teachers been more approachable.

> Kevin was in the infant age group at the time of his parent's death. Kevin reported that his teachers adopted a very formal approach. Kevin was told by one of his teachers to 'keep a stiff upper lip old chap!', a remark which seemed to be far more appropriate at Rorke's Drift or Dunkirk, than to an infant youngster.

The response of that teacher, as perhaps with Tina's teachers, may be because they did not know what to say to him. There were similar reports from older children.

> Rory was a teenager at the time of his father's death, and he remarked that talking to the teachers at the school about the death was never 'on the agenda'; it was as if it was an unwritten rule at his school. Rory felt quite isolated at school after the death of his father.

Sarah was also a teenager at the time of the death of her mother. Sarah described how the teachers at her school did not seem to be at all interested in the death, and it was if her mother had never existed. Sarah found this lack of interest very hard to understand and come to terms with.

As with the experiences of many other volunteers, the reality for their teachers may have been that they either did not know how to respond, or else were wary of causing an upset.

Natasha said that she was far too scared to approach her teachers after the death of her father, even though she would have liked to have talked things through with somebody at her school.

Some volunteers were unwilling to seek help at school: one-tenth of them said that they did not want to approach their teachers, and would not have welcomed being approached by their teachers. In contrast, many of the volunteers would have welcomed and been helped by an approach. Teachers are adults and it seems strange that they seemed unable to make the first move and initiate potentially helpful interactions with the children. This may reflect the nature of death as taboo and also the possible fear that the teachers may have of crossing the professional boundary to become involved in an emotional transaction with their pupils. There was no clear linear relationship between the ages of the volunteers and the approachability of their teachers, as shown in Table 13.2.

Table 13.2 The volunteers, by age group, finding their teachers approachable					
Pre-school	5–7 yr	8–11 yr	12–15 yr	16+ yr	Overall
0%	13%	4%	8%	0%	6%

The Iceberg volunteers in the infant age group generally found their teachers to be the most approachable. The pre-school and the older secondary aged teachers were found to be the least approachable by the volunteers. The overall results are perhaps not surprising, as the volunteers had already generally reported that they did not find that their school helped them on their return after the death of their parent.

Who the Iceberg volunteers spoke with about their feelings relating to the death of their parent

The general picture emerging is that the volunteers were tending to receive little support at their schools, and many of them had feelings of being isolated and ignored and also that they did not find their teachers at all approachable. Over two thirds of the Iceberg volunteers thought that their schools did nothing to help them on their return, and a similar number thought that teachers were not approachable. The volunteers were next asked if they spoke to anybody else about their feelings revolving around the death of their parent; the results are shown in Table 13.3.

Table 13.3 Who the volunteers spoke with about their feelings

	%
Nobody	56
Close friend(s)	20
Siblings	13
Mother	11
Grandmother	4
Family friend	3
Father	3

Just over half the volunteers said that they spoke with nobody about their feelings and experiences, in the time after the death of their parent.

Charles was in his teens at the time of the death of his father. Charles described his most disconcerting memory being that everyone seemed to be giving him a wide berth and even his friends and acquaintances seemed to be actively avoiding him, even on the level of social chit-chat.

Those volunteers who did talk with somebody sometimes had more than one confidant. One-fifth of the volunteers spoke to friends. Just over one-ninth of the volunteers confided only in their mother.

There was a slight sex difference in that 58 per cent of the female volunteers spoke to nobody, compared to 52 per cent of the males. The percentage of the sexes speaking only to friends was similar, although more of the females confided in their mothers than did the males. While 13 per cent of the volunteers spoke with their siblings, only a small minority spoke to their grandmother and their father.

> Tim was a young teenager at the death of his father. Tim was able to speak only to a psychiatrist after the death; sadly there was nobody else with whom he could talk, only a relatively short time after the death.

The majority of the Iceberg volunteers did not talk to anybody at all about their feelings, and this seemed to reinforce their general impression of being isolated and ignored at school and at home. Those volunteers who did speak with somebody generally confided in just one person, who was usually a close friend, sibling or their mother. This suggests that the grief of the volunteers when they were children was generally not being facilitated by the adults around them.

> Luke was a young teenager at the time of his mother's death and found that his father would just not talk about things at all. In the medium and long term this made Luke quite angry and the relationship with his father broke down.

Did any other adults help the Iceberg volunteers?

Did the volunteers find that other adults in their life were easy to talk to, and did they help to facilitate their grieving? Two-thirds of the volunteers did not find other adults at all easy to approach; these were nearly three-quarters of the female volunteers and over half of the males. One-tenth of the females said that they did not want to talk to anybody else about the death, a response not reported by any of the males. Nearly one-eighth of the Iceberg volunteers said that they did find adults easy to approach; this was one-fifth of the males and just under one-tenth of the females.

Some volunteers said that there was variation in the response of adults whom they did approach to talk about the death, some being more approachable than others. This does not seem surprising, as some individuals are more comfortable than others in talking about death.

Many volunteers seemed to be as isolated at home as they were at their school. This supports the notion that some of the difficulties which families and children encounter after bereavement are partly related to their poor communication around the topic of death (Pattison 1976). The volunteers had generally reported that they had felt quite isolated at their schools and that their teachers were not at all easily approached, and also that the other adults in their life were also not easy to talk with about the death. It seems hardly surprising that such a level of isolation was reported, considering that the volunteers seemed to have little support. Many volunteers found that the difficulty which they had at the time in talking about their feelings has continued into the longer term, and that they still as adults tend to bottle up their emotions and not talk to others. Some volunteers still had difficulties talking with their parents.

> Dick was 13 at the time of his dad's sudden death, and he told how he had tried to talk about things with his mother several times. The discussion always broke down and ended in arguments, as the whole subject of the death seemed to be so emotionally charged.

Chapter 14

The Iceberg volunteers' feelings over the two year period after the death of their parents

The Iceberg volunteers were asked to report on their experiences over a series of time periods after the death of their parent:

- one month after the death of their parent
- six months after the death
- one year after the death
- two years after the death.

How the Iceberg volunteers were feeling a month after the death of their parent

The volunteers were asked to say how they felt a month after the death of their parent. At this time, the funeral would have taken place and the vast majority of them had returned to their schools. Not all of the volunteers could recall the events at that time, and Table 14.1 shows the Iceberg volunteers, by age group, who said that they could not remember the events a month after the death of their parent.

Table 14.1 The volunteers, by age group, with 'no recall' a month after the death of their parent					
Pre-school	5–7 yr	8–11 yr	12–15 yr	16+ yr	Total
60%	50%	24%	7%	0%	21%

There was a relationship between the age of the volunteers at the death of their parent and their ability to recall events at the time a month after the death of their parent. The percentage of volunteers reporting that they were unable to recall events a month after the death decreased with their age. All the Iceberg volunteers in the oldest age group could recall the events. Two-thirds of the volunteers in the pre-school group could not recall the events.

Intuitively it does seem reasonable to assume that there would be a relationship between the age of the volunteer and their ability to recall events. One-third of the males and one-fifth of the females said that they had no recall of events at this time. I considered that the relatively high rates of Iceberg volunteers saying that they had no recall was not problematic, but rather a reflection of the honesty of the volunteers in reporting. It is not possible to verify the reliability of the recall of the volunteers at the time, although for many, the event of the death of their parent and the surrounding circumstances seemed etched in their minds. The main reactions recalled by the volunteers varied. One-fifth of the volunteers said that they were feeling normal.

One-fifth of the volunteers could not remember either events or their feelings a month after the death of their parent, and these were removed from the data. A quarter of the volunteers reported being in shock at the time; another quarter said that they were feeling defensive. Many volunteers described how they felt that they 'had a shield up' as children at that time.

It was remarkable that so many of them chose to use the word 'shield', which gives a visual image of them being quite defensive. One-fifth of the volunteers, all males, said that they were now feeling normal at this time. Normality was reported by one-third of the male group and was an unexpected reaction. There was no difference whether it was their mother or their father who had died.

Other feelings reported by the Iceberg volunteers a month after the death of their parent included isolation (one-eighth), sadness (one-eighth), and anger and guilt (one-tenth and one-twentieth respectively). About 4 per cent of the volunteers said that they were feeling quite depressed at that time. All the feelings reported by the volunteers feature in the traditional models of loss, although the initial stages of these traditional models tend to focus on the feelings of shock. Feelings such as anger, guilt and depression feature only in the later stages of the traditional models, and the idea of normality reported at such an early stage after a death is neither part of the stage nor task models.

Normality in terms of the stage model is thought of as the resolution of the loss, and in terms of the task model, when the tasks of mourning have been completed. It is often thought that grieving in the stage or task models takes around two years to complete.

Although this question was intended to focus on the volunteers' emotional responses at the time of the death, there were other surprising answers. The volunteers frequently mentioned other things that had happened at this time, beyond emotional responses, but events that had made an impact on them at the time. One in fourteen of the Iceberg volunteers had already moved house. This came as a surprise as it was only a month since the death of their parent. Some volunteers told how they moved long distances soon after the death, and were often subject to teasing for now having different accents from the rest of the children. Sasha and Emily were two volunteers who moved soon after the death of their fathers:

> Sasha was 8 years old when her father died, and related how she was 'whisked off' away from her home straight after her father's funeral, for a new life with grandparents in another and strange part of the country. This she described as being a complete culture change and shock, and with the move of house came other changes, such as neighbourhood, friends and school.

> Emily was at junior school when her father died, and she told how all her beloved family pets were 'destroyed' at that time. The family quickly moved away after the death, and the pets could not be taken with them, nor were they found alternative homes.

Both Sasha and Emily were experiencing further losses, beyond the death of their fathers. Many volunteers experienced and reported similar losses, which were flowing directly as a result of the death of their parent. These were surprising, and had not been anticipated, especially so close to the death of the parent. Just under one-tenth of the volunteers reported experiencing what they described as 'family problems', which included friction, tension and arguments within the family at home. These difficulties seemed to relate to the change in dynamics within the family now that one of the parents was dead, as well as to grieving relating to the death. One volunteer spoke of having what he described as a 'nervous breakdown'; he was already receiving psychiatric support at this time, only shortly after the death of his parent. There were other reports of regression, such as bedwetting, by junior aged volunteers who had long since ceased to have such difficulties, until the death.

The death of the parent seemed, unsurprisingly, to be taking an emotional strain on the remaining family members, in terms of their grief, but it was also beginning to have an impact on the family in practical terms, flowing directly from the parental death. This seemed to have the potential to compound further the emotional difficulties of the children. Imagine the feelings of Emily, who had to cope not only with the death of her father and the sudden move of her home but also with the 'destruction' of her pets. Emily also had a change of school to contend with, involving the loss of her classmates and the teachers she knew well. All these subsequent events were themselves losses, adding to that already caused by the death of the parent.

Things had now changed irrevocably for many of the Iceberg volunteers, not only in terms of the death of their parent, but also in terms of other life changes that were beginning to flow as a direct result of the effects of the parental death.

A small minority of the males now said that they hated their school at this particular time. This may have been an apparent expression of anger relating not only to the death of their parent but also to the lack of response by their school. Other volunteers said that they became quite rebellious at this time, and some said how they were then feeling quite bitter and angry. These seem to have been at least partly related to unfacilitated grieving, which may have been helped by some sort of intervention at that time. Other volunteers said that their family was now having problems with money, these being economic difficulties associated with the death of their parent. One of the breadwinners in the family had now died, and there were also other costs, such as the funeral expenses, which now had to be paid.

Richard said that because of the new economic circumstances after his father's death, his mum then had to go out to work, and that things were never the same again.

Paula found that the practicalities surrounding single parent living were starting to dominate, and it was this that she found depressing. Paula's mother now left for work early in the morning and the children were faced with coming home to an empty house and waiting for her return.

The reports suggest that the experiences of the volunteers when they were children were beginning to deviate from those of the adult based traditional models.

How the Iceberg volunteers were feeling six months after the death of their parents

The Iceberg volunteers were next asked to recall how they felt six months after the death of their parent.

- One-quarter of the volunteers reported feeling depressed at that time.

- One-fifth of the volunteers now said that they were feeling normal.

- Just over one-tenth of the volunteers said that the reality of the death had now 'hit them' at this time.

- One-tenth of the volunteers said that they now felt quite isolated.

Nearly one-third of the males and one-sixth of the females reported that they could not recall events from that time. There was little difference in the rate of recall reported by the volunteers between the periods of a month and six months after the death. The number of volunteers able to recall had now nearly halved from the initial time of the death, although this is perhaps not a surprise, considering the likely impact that the news initially would have had, and therefore more likely to be remembered.

In the one-quarter of volunteers who said that they were feeling depressed, there were no significant sex differences. The one-fifth of volunteers who reported what they described as 'normality' at this time comprised nearly one-third of the males and one-tenth of the females. Just over one-tenth of the volunteers, all females, reported that there were family problems, and so relatively soon after the death of their partner, one in twenty of the surviving parents had remarried. There were likely to have been other new and less formal arrangements, some perhaps unrecognised by the volunteers.

> June was a teenager when her dad died and found that soon after the death her mum introduced a new boyfriend into the family. June was now expected to cook for her mum's new man, with whom she did not have a good relationship. This also had a detrimental effect on the relationship she had with her mum.

Other volunteers said that they found their parent's new and sometimes temporary relationships quite difficult to understand at the time. There seems to have been a feeling that the parent was being disloyal to their dead spouse.

There were other interesting differences in the reports of the volunteers six months after the death compared with a month after the death of their parent. Reports by the Iceberg volunteers of sadness, shock, anger and defensiveness had declined. Reports of depression by the volunteers had increased. The reporting of shock had reduced from one-third of the volunteers a month after the death to one-ninth at six months. The reports of being defensive, which included the 'shields up' reaction reported by some volunteers, had declined from one-third of the volunteers a month after the death to less than one-tenth six months later.

In contrast, reports of depression by the Iceberg volunteers had been mentioned by only 4 per cent of the volunteers a month after the death, but it was now being reported by nearly 25 per cent of all those who were able to recall events from this time. In the traditional models of grieving, depression is the stage following shock, although the more flexible models do allow for movement between the stages. Another unexpected result was that one-third of the male volunteers said that they were feeling 'normal' at this time, compared with one-tenth of the females. In the traditional models, normality is generally considered as when the bereaved individual reaches the stage of 'resolution', taking up to two years after the death. More of the male than female volunteers reported feelings of normality at this time, although more of the males were also feeling depressed. Only 4 per cent of the males said that they were still in shock at this time, whereas 16 per cent of the females still said that they were either in shock or had feelings of 'unreality' about the death of their parent.

There were still more reports of significant life changes for some of the Iceberg volunteers, bringing yet more life changes and further additional losses, and again I had not anticipated these changes being reported so soon after the death.

One-tenth of the Iceberg volunteers had either moved house with their family or had gone to live with other relations who lived well away from their former home. These volunteers, when they were children, had lost their homes, friends and social contacts in the area, as well as their schools, teachers and classmates. Their new school would have been unlikely to have any links with the family or the children. The move of school would probably be unlikely to improve the response of the school to either the family or to the child. The new teachers of the volunteers may have assumed that characteristics, such as expressions of anger or moodiness, were more personality based 'in child' factors rather than being contextually based as a grief reaction.

One in twenty-five of the Iceberg volunteers had already experienced their surviving parent remarrying. The arrival of a new adult partner in a family must have had at least some marginal effect on the dynamics. This could well have a major impact, as the children may have had feelings of loyalty for their dead parent, and perhaps regard the new partner as an intruder. The new partner may well cater for some of the emotional and other needs of the surviving parent, but not necessarily for those of the children. The Iceberg volunteers would now have also lost at least a part of the remaining parent, in that their attention and focus will now be at least marginally directed elsewhere.

One in seven of the Iceberg volunteers said that they were now experiencing other family changes, problems and difficulties, which they perceived as being directly related to the death of their parent. Many volunteers were now reporting that the reality of the death of their parent had now hit home, suggesting that the initial shock phase or inability to take in the fact of the death had now ended. The parental death had now perhaps had more of an impact cognitively on the volunteers, something that was not mentioned previously. The volunteers seem to have been moving towards revised schema or mind-sets, which were changing, integrating within it the death of their parent. There had perhaps been a period of transition from the old life schema to the revised and new schema of life.

As noted, the reports of depression by the volunteers had increased over this time, as had the number reporting normality. There was clearly some movement towards normality, as also indicated by those volunteers reporting the increased awareness of reality. There is a difference between the reports of 'normality' and of 'reality hitting home'. The latter reports by the volunteers would seem to be part of the process of moving towards the former. It would seem to have been difficult for the volunteers to report the condition of normality without implicitly having had accepted the reality of the situation, that being the death of their parent.

Throughout this six month period, the remaining parent too would have been going through their own period of grieving and adjustment, and they may not have been fully able to facilitate their children's own grieving.

It was at this stage that third level losses, caused by the second level changes, were being reported. For example, after the death, there may no longer have been a mum at home after school. She may have died, or in the case of a paternal death, have needed to take up employment outside the home. The remaining parent would be unlikely to oversee or control the children as effectively as when there were two parents.

The outcomes for the Iceberg volunteers were sometimes quite different in similar circumstances, and this seemed to have related to their own personality and inner resources. Some volunteers became quite resourceful and independent after the death of their parent. These particular volunteers said that they grew up very quickly, and felt that they were stronger from the experience of the bereavement. They perceived that they gained a measure of much valued independence, when they compared themselves to their peers, whom they thought were relatively immature.

Carl was a teenager at the time of his dad's death and felt that he was left to fend for himself far more than his peers with two parents. Carl's view was that many of his peers were quite babyish and he valued that he had far more independence, simply because his mum could not always be about, as she had before the death.

Jason said how, on reflection, he had been like a 13 year old 'going on 20' after the death of his father. Jason began smoking and drinking and described himself as a 'brat' at the time.

This could be quite a positive outcome, although the volunteers had also partly lost their childhood through losing some measure of the parental screen. One in twenty-five of the Iceberg volunteers said that they had now begun to focus on their academic work. In contrast, other volunteers did not have such positive reports about school. One in sixteen of the volunteers said that there had been a decline in their academic attainments. The only previous mention of academic work by any of the Iceberg volunteers was that some of them had said that it had become harder, a month after the death of the parent. This was perhaps an indication of a decline in concentration, perhaps preoccupation and depression after the death. It may be that children tend to be so preoccupied after a parental death, that they lack a focus of attention for their work at school. In contrast it could be that some children immerse themselves in their work at school after a parental death (Knapman 1993).

There were reports of rebellious behaviour by some volunteers, and these reports continued to increase over time. This rebellion seems to stem from an anger response after the death of their parent, and perhaps a generic protest against the perceived unfairness of life. This may also have related to the apparent lack of facilitation of the children's grieving. Anger is also an element in the traditional models of grieving. The rebellion of the Iceberg volunteers may also have related to the understandable reduction in parenting management, especially at a time when the surviving parent would be struggling with their own grief.

> Mike was a pre-schooler at the time of his father's death, and he can recall that both himself and his brother were quite naughty, even wild at the time following the death of his father. Mike's mother found the pair very difficult to cope with at the time, and the brothers were partly looked after by elderly relatives.

Mike said that fortunately the boys eventually calmed down, through the intervention and support of a kindly retired teacher. They could easily have been drawn into less desirable company, with far more negative outcomes for them both. Jason also thought that his perceived lack of a good education was directly related to the death of his father. Two females said that they were now helping their mothers much more after the death of their fathers. In one way they both felt that they were becoming more independent and responsible, but in another way they were not having the space of childhood, something which many such as Donna regretted having missed.

> Donna was a teenager at the time of her mum's death and was in effect forced into being a quasi partner for her father. Donna had to take the role of caring for the younger children of the family, being a substitute for her mother. This role was not at all relished by Donna and she left home as soon as she could after the death to make her own way independently.

There were adverse repercussions in Donna's subsequent relationship with both her father and siblings, which stemmed from the death. Carrie too found that the death of her father and her mother's subsequent remarriage led her to leave home:

> Carrie was a teenager at the time of her father's death and felt that her mother and her new husband had made a new

life together of which she was not really part. She did feel that this led to her going to college, something that she may not have done.

Other volunteers were involved in more sinister consequences:

Paula was also a teenager at the time that her father died and she fell prey sexually to a 'friend' of the family. Paula said that she was quite misled and taken advantage of by the family 'friend' yet she dared not share these difficulties with the rest of the family, who were quite puzzled by her subsequent shunning of the 'friend'.

Paula had experienced yet another loss after the death of her father, and was convinced that this would not have happened had he not died. Her perception was that the further loss was a consequence of the death. In addition, Paula chose to keep the incident to herself, to avoid what she thought would be giving more upsetting news to her family, although was not sure at the time whether she would have been believed. Iceberg volunteers reported still having nightmares and flashbacks relating to the death of their parent, and some of them said that they were still in quite a confused state at this time.

The volunteers were now really deviating from the traditional models of loss, in particular in relation to the reporting of normality which seemed premature, but also in respect of some being in a state of shock and confusion. The growing reports of depression at the time were in line with the traditional models.

How the Iceberg volunteers were feeling a year after the death of their parents

The third point in time at which the volunteers were asked to recall how they were was a year after the death of their parent. The first anniversary of a death is usually significant for the bereaved, and adults whom I have counselled often approach this first anniversary with a great deal of trepidation. There often seem to be very powerful contextual cues potentially bringing back memories, especially if the death had taken place at an evocative time such as Christmas, or the summer holidays.

The number of Iceberg volunteers who were now unable to recall events fell by half to around one-tenth compared with the six month period. Perhaps the volunteers were more able to relate to the anniversary, through contextual clues. One-third of the volunteers were now reporting feelings of normality, suggesting that some of them, at least to a degree, had come to terms with the death of their parent. It may be that the new circumstances of life were now integrated within their mind-sets. The traditional stage and task models of loss would suggest that this is a relatively short time for this 'normality' to have taken place, as two years is generally thought of as a more appropriate period for the resolution of grief. A difficulty is deciding what exactly 'resolution' means. It tends to be used in the sense that the death no longer impacts on the life of the individual to the degree that it interferes with their everyday life. The bereaved are then described as being able to move on, and invest their energy elsewhere. This could be perhaps what the volunteers were describing as feeling 'normal' when they were children. They would still have had memories of their parent, and would not deny moments of both memory and sadness, but to a large extent they had adapted themselves to their new circumstances. This does suggest quite a degree of resilience within the volunteers.

An interesting feature is that the number of male volunteers now reporting normality was very similar to the six month period. In contrast, the number of female volunteers reporting normality increased from 10 per cent at six months to one-third a year after the death of the parent. The intervening six month period seems to have been crucial for many females in terms of their adjustment to the death of their parent.

There were now also reports of antisocial and potentially self-harming behaviour from the Iceberg volunteers. Substance abuse was now reported by 4 per cent of the volunteers, and others reported truanting, lack of confidence and other problems.

> Clara, who was in her teens at the time of the death of her parent, described how she had begun to binge on food. With hindsight Clara considered that she was very close to having an eating disorder.

> Rita became quite concerned after the death of her father that her mum might also die. Rita kept a close watch on her mum, waiting for her return whenever she went out on any short trip, such as to the shops. At the time Rita always wanted to know her mum's whereabouts.

The behaviours of both these young women seem to reflect both anxiety and insecurity, a basic distrust of life, as well as perhaps Clara now having low feelings of self-worth. It is not, of course, possible to know whether these behaviours would have occurred without the death of the volunteer's parent, but it was clear that they themselves saw a connection between these subsequent problems and the death of their parent. These results do fit in with the evidence of drug abuse seeming to result from children's unresolved grief after a parental death (Lamers 1986).

The number of volunteers reporting depression had now declined to one in seven, from the one in four reporting it six months earlier. This could be an indication of the volunteers moving through the stages of grief. The incidence of isolation reported by the volunteers doubled in this time period, and now one in seven of them felt isolated. Again, half as many again females than males said that they had such feelings. There was also a marginal increase in the Iceberg volunteers who said that they were angry, this was mentioned by just a few more of the volunteers, about half the number reporting feeling angry when hearing the news of the death.

One-tenth of the volunteers now reported feelings of sadness, a feeling which was not mentioned at all at the six month period, and it had now returned close to the level it was a month after the death of the parent. The reporting of sadness was equally spread across the ages and sexes. This supports the view that the anniversary of the death, especially the first anniversary, is a difficult time for bereaved people in general. The volunteers may well have picked up and reflected sadness from the adults who were around them at the time. It is difficult to conclude that the volunteers, as young children, would themselves have remembered the date of the death, unless there were very strong cues, such as it being close to Christmas, a birthday, or at the start of the summer holidays. The triggers for the volunteers may well therefore have been the reactions of the adults around them. The feelings of isolation may also have been triggered by the memories of the parent's death a year earlier.

Another 3 per cent of the Iceberg volunteers had moved house over this second six month period, and nearly 20 per cent had moved in the period up to the first anniversary. Moving house leads to the likelihood of further losses as related earlier. Other volunteers reported that their parent had now remarried, making a total of 6 per cent during the first year after the death. There may also have been other, perhaps less formal, arrangements, which would have impacted to a greater or lesser degree on the volunteers when they were children.

One in seven of the volunteers, all females, reported general family problems at this time, and there were obviously stresses and strains within some of the family systems. It may be that the male volunteers were either just not aware of these difficulties or else that they had distanced themselves emotionally away from the family. One in fourteen of the Iceberg volunteers now said that they were having economic problems at the time; all these were where fathers had died, and the subsequent loss of income was now making an impact on the family. It seemed that the full impact of the effects of the bereavement, in terms of these second and third level losses, were now beginning to have a greater effect on the volunteers and their families.

One-tenth of the volunteers, all females, reported an actual improvement in their academic work at school, in direct contrast to the one-twentieth who reported a decrease in their academic work. The reactions of some volunteers may have been to throw themselves into their academic work. Others, perhaps through being more depressed, seemed to have either lost interest or not seen the point of academic work, and this was reflected in a decrease in their work at school.

There were now no reports by any volunteers of them either being defensive or of the reality hitting home. This suggests that they had all now absorbed the impact of what had happened, although one in fourteen still report that they were in shock. The experiences of the volunteers seemed in some ways to mirror the traditional models of grief, although, as mentioned before, the reports of normality would not usually be anticipated just one year after a death.

How the Iceberg volunteers were feeling two years after the death of their parents

The final time at which the volunteers were asked to recall their feelings was two years after their parent's death. This was again an anniversary of the death, although with perhaps not quite the same impact as the first one.

There was a marginal increase in the frequency of volunteers now reporting that they were 'feeling normal' at the second anniversary of the death: nearly four in ten of those Iceberg volunteers who were able to recall events. Nearly half of the females now said that they were feeling normal, double the rate of the males.

During the early stages in the time after the death, more of the male volunteers had reported feelings of normality, and their reports had remained similar over the previous two time points. In contrast, reports by the females had now increased to be around twice that of the males. It may be that many males felt that they had recovered from the death of their parent quite quickly at first, whereas for the females it was a much slower process.

The traditional models of loss would suggest that most of the bereaved would have come to the resolution of their grief by this time. In contrast, two-thirds of the volunteers did not report normality after two years, suggesting that for the majority, reaching the stage of 'resolution' took longer than a period of two years. This is perhaps not surprising in terms of the earlier reports made by the Iceberg volunteers.

- Many volunteers had felt quite isolated and excluded both at their school and home.

- Many volunteers had found neither their teachers nor the other adults in their lives approachable.

- Many volunteers did not take part in the traditional rituals after the death of their parent, such as visiting the chapel of rest or attending the funeral.

Volunteers who had attended the funeral were generally quite positive about the experience, and the results for the chapel of rest, while not so conclusive, were overall quite positive. This would seem to support the notion that many children do need adult support in order to resolve their grief, and this did not seem to have been happening for many of the Iceberg volunteers. It is therefore perhaps not a surprise that so many had not fully come to terms with the death of their parent at this time.

One-seventh of the volunteers said that they were feeling depressed at that time, a similar number to the first anniversary. There was an increase in the reports of anger, which had doubled to one in fourteen of the volunteers. Sadness had also slightly declined as a report by volunteers, from one in ten to one in seventeen over this period, and the percentage of the volunteers feeling isolated was similar comparing the first and second anniversaries of the parental death.

Perhaps the greatest change over this time period was in those volunteers reporting feeling shock. None of the volunteers reported shock at the second anniversary of the death, compared to one-quarter a month after the death. This decline fits in with the traditional stage model of loss, where shock is regarded as one of the initial reactions. It also fits in with the task model of loss, where the initial task is to accept the reality of the loss, implying that the shock of the death has to have been worked through by the bereaved.

Although no volunteers reported having moved house during the intervening year, just over one-twentieth said that their parent now had a new partner. This meant that now one-seventh of the volunteers had experienced their surviving parent having a new partner, with further changes and losses for the volunteers having already experienced the death of a parent.

One in fourteen of the Iceberg volunteers said that they were now putting a focus on either their academic work at school, or else on sport, being a positive distractor for them. In contrast, another fourteenth of the volunteers said that they now either hated school, or that they had no interest at all in their work at school. There was a sex difference in the reports: some of the male volunteers said that they hated school, while some of the female volunteers said that they experienced a loss of interest in school.

There was another difference in the responses of the sexes: the male volunteers had an anger type response, while the female volunteers had more of a depressed type response. Some of the males whose father had died were now truanting from school. There were no reports of either females or males whose mothers had died truanting at this time. This was an interesting finding and it may have been connected with the loss of their role model or else the inability of their mothers to control or resolve this type of activity. This time was also one where some volunteers felt that things had become clear.

> Carol was at primary school when her father had died, and she characterised the period ending with the second anniversary of the death as the time when the fuller implications of the death came home to her. Until that time, Carol felt that she had not really understood the full implications of the death.

Other volunteers reported that they were feeling odd, independent or guilty. Some volunteers had felt that they were different, from the initial time of the news of the death, and in many ways they were different from their peers who had not been through the experience of a parental death. A minority of the volunteers still reported that they had nightmares, were fearful or perceived that they were being bullied.

Summary of the Iceberg volunteers' feelings and experiences for the two year period following the death of their parents

Table 14.2 summarises the main reactions of the volunteers over the two year period from the death of their parent. The figures are percentages of the volunteers reporting the particular reaction.

Table 14.2 Summary, as percentages, of the major reactions of the volunteers over the initial two year period after the death of their parent				
Reaction	I month	6 months	I year	2 years
Shock	24	11	7	0
Defensiveness	24	6	0	0
No recall	21	19	11	13
Normality	14	17	33	34
Isolation	10	7	11	11
Sadness	10	0	9	6
Anger	7	1	3	7
Moved house	6	9	3	0
Guilt	4	4	3	1
Depression	3	19	14	14
Reality hit	0	9	0	0

The volunteers' initial reactions to the death of their parent, from those who could recall the events at the time, were that they were unable to absorb the information fully. The impact of the death was perhaps just too great for volunteers to take in at the time as children, and this does seem to mirror the adult experience in the traditional models of grieving.

Recall of events

One-tenth of the volunteers could not recall their initial reaction to the news of the death. This inability to recall events rose to one-quarter a month later, and declined to one-fifth at the time six months after the death. Interestingly, the 'no recall' group of volunteers reduced to one-tenth on the first anniversary of the death, the same amount as at the time of first hearing the news of the death, at the second anniversary. Several volunteers suggested that this period in their life may have been so difficult that they had just blanked it out of their lives.

Shock and defensiveness

One-quarter of the Iceberg volunteers said they were in shock a month after the death of their parent, with a similar number reporting that they were defensive and had their 'shields up'. These were the two main feelings at the one month period, although a not insignificant one-fifth of the volunteers said that they felt what they described as normal. The defensive response declined substantially after six months to one-sixteenth of the volunteers. The reports of shock fell from one-quarter of the volunteers at the month period, to one-ninth after six months, to one in fourteen a year after the death, and finally to disappear as a report after two years.

Normality

One-seventh of the Iceberg volunteers reported feelings of normality a month after the death, increasing to one-third at the second anniversary of the death.

Sadness

One-tenth of the Iceberg volunteers reported sadness as their main feeling one month after the death of their parent. Sadness was not reported at all by any volunteers after six months, although it did reappear as a response by nearly one-tenth of the volunteers at the first anniversary, declining to one-sixteenth two years after the death of their parent. It could well be that the anniversaries of the deaths revived the initial feelings of sadness.

Anger

Anger was reported by one-fourteenth of the volunteers a month after the death, although only by males. The reports of anger then declined to a nominal level after six months, rising to one-thirtieth after a year and then to one-fourteenth two years after the death. The reports of anger seemed to be increasing as those of sadness had declined. This may have related to a growing conceptual awareness of what had happened or as a response to subsequent events that followed the death of the parent.

Depression

Depression was reported by only 3 per cent of the Iceberg volunteers a month after the death, rising to one-fifth after six months. Depression then seemed to reach a plateau of one in seven at the first anniversary of the death, falling marginally at the end of the second year. In the traditional models of loss, depression is generally considered to be a later rather than an earlier response to a death. This was the case with the Iceberg study.

Guilt

There was very little evidence of feelings of guilt reported by the volunteers, in contrast to the traditional models. This is not really surprising, as the children tended to have very little control or power over the events that followed the death of their parent, especially as compared to the surrounding adult. In these circumstances, guilt would not really be an expected response. The reports of guilt by the Iceberg volunteers was at its highest level (4%), both one month and six months after the death of the parent. The reports fell to nominal levels after one and two years.

Some volunteers expressed regret at being excluded from family events such as visiting their parent in the chapel of rest or attending the funeral, but this regret was not reflected in feelings of guilt.

Summary

The patterns of grieving that emerged from the stories of the Iceberg volunteers seemed far too complex to be dealt with by a simple stage model. There were a relatively high number of volunteers who reported feeling 'normal' quite soon after the death of their parent, and having adapted to the new situation. This suggests either a high level of resilience or tenacity within the Iceberg volunteers as a group, or else that they were in some ways processing the loss quite differently from adults.

Males in particular initially reported a higher level of normality than did the females. The rate of normality reported by the females was, however, twice that of the males by the second anniversary of the death. Despite these indications of resilience among some volunteers, two-thirds of the volunteers had not reached the stage of normality two years after the death of their parent. The two year period is a rule of thumb and frequently used in predicting the resolution of grief.

For some Iceberg volunteers, when they were children there was a return to normality. In contrast, for many others there were the second or third level losses, not directly related to the breaking of the bonding relationship with their parent, but connected with further life changes resulting from the death. The changes for the volunteers included moving house, district or school, or the arrival of a new partner for their parent.

Chapter 15

The medium and long-term effects of the death of their parents on the Iceberg volunteers

Introduction

The Iceberg volunteers had been asked about their feelings and how they were at various points after the death of their parent, on five specific occasions:

- on first hearing the news of the death of their parent
- one month after the death
- six months after the death
- one year after the death
- two years after the death.

These times were chosen as it was thought that the volunteers were likely to have a reasonable recall of events for then. The death of the parents also potentially seemed to be having far-reaching effects, and part of Iceberg was to track the medium and long-term effects on the lives of the volunteers. This was also to look for effects beyond the traditional two year period of grieving, the time when the conventional wisdom would seem to suggest that the bereaved individual would have 'recovered' from their loss. This does not mean that the volunteers would no longer have memories of their dead parent, but that the effects of the death would no longer impact on their daily lives. The volunteers were asked to report on difficulties they experienced after the death but in the medium and longer term. The volunteers were specifically asked to mention only things that they considered related to the death of their parent.

- Over one-fifth of the Iceberg volunteers said that they had experienced delayed grief.

- Over one-fifth of the volunteers said that they had their own relationship difficulties.

- Over one-fifth of the volunteers said that they had feelings of vulnerability.

- Over one-fifth of the volunteers said that they had long-term depression.

- Over one-tenth of the volunteers said that they had later sought a psychiatric referral.

- One-tenth of the volunteers said that they had what they described as 'separation anxiety'.

- One-tenth of the volunteers said that they had no confidence.

One of the difficulties with the answers to this question is that these longer-term effects of the parental death could well be both underestimated and underreported. Conversely, the effects could even be overestimated. The Iceberg volunteers may have been set on a totally different life trajectory after the death of their parent, and they may not have connected all these changes with the death. The volunteers may not even have been aware of some of the implications or ramifications of the death. Conversely the volunteers could perhaps falsely connect an event with the bereavement. They may perhaps mistakenly perceive that their own later relationship difficulties were related to the death of their parent. It is very difficult to 'unpack' these longer-term changes, although the things reported were, for the volunteers, their reality of the events. On average each volunteer reported just under three longer-term effects that they considered were of significance and also which they considered had related directly from the death of their parent.

Delayed grief

One-third of the females reported delayed and unresolved grief, as did one in ten of the males, an interesting difference between the sexes. The volunteers considered that, even some time after the death of their parent, they had still not fully resolved their grief, and had not reached the stage of 'resolution'. Both Frances and Margaret's stories are typical of many of those told by Iceberg volunteers.

> Frances was 12 years old when her mother died and she said that she still actively avoided mother and daughter and family situations, and at the time tended to find friendships with other children from single parent families where the mother had also died. She also found that her own relationships were very problematic. Frances felt that becoming 'too close' to a man was difficult in terms of potentially being emotionally hurt in the long run.

I did find during the search for volunteers that many of those taking part had contacts with others who were in a similar position, and in a sense they had formed mutually supporting groups who could both identify and empathise with each other. It was felt that those who had not gone through the experience could not really fully understand.

> Margaret was a teenager at the time of her father's sudden death, and she reflected that she also found relationships

very hard to cope with, and that she tended to 'bottle things up' rather than 'deal with them'.

It may be that having gone through the experience of a parent's death, both Frances and Margaret always expected the worst to happen, and that they felt that any happiness in terms of a relationship could easily vanish, as had their parent.

Bruce was 8 at the time of his father's death and told how he became quite jealous of children from 'normal' families with both parents. Bruce tended to seek the company of other children who also had only one parent, through death or the separation of their parents.

Children may well experience delayed grieving, and it may take them a longer time than adults to resolve their grief (Hemmings 1995). The results of Iceberg in general do support this for the majority of the volunteers, although a minority considered that they resolved their grief relatively quickly. The delay in grieving may have related to the lack of help and facilitation that the volunteers, as children, could obtain from adults (Raphael 1984). The volunteers generally did not think that they had received much help or support either at school or at home, from the adults in their lives. This may be a reason why the volunteers' patterns of grieving did seem to differ, at least in some ways, from the traditional models of loss.

Long-term depression

One in five volunteers reported having long-term depression. This suggests that the 'recovery' or 'resolution' stage had not yet been reached for these volunteers.

Hazel was 10 years old when her father died, and she said that she was still depressed about the death when she went to college several years later, such was the impact that the death had made on her, and so lacking was the support.

One-third of the females and one-tenth of the males reported having this longer-term depression. The female volunteers seemed far more likely to have long-term problems with unresolved grief and depression than were the males. One in sixteen volunteers, all females and all after the deaths of their fathers, said that they had now become quite 'inward looking'. This suggests that they too may well have been on the depression continuum and over one-third of all female volunteers were displaying some form of longer-term depression. This may suggest an apparent link between depressive illness in the adult life of women, and their earlier maternal bereavement (Brown *et al.* 1977; Hill 1969). Although medium and long-term depression was reported by a greater percentage of the female volunteers, there was no correlation between the ages of the volunteers at the death of their parent and depression. Iceberg does not support the idea of the early teenage years being a particularly vulnerable time for females in connection with parental death and longer-term depression. There were no differences in the reports of longer-term depression and as to whether the death was maternal or paternal. The female volunteers in Iceberg reported the same rates of depression whether the death was that of their mother or of their father, there was no link between the death of a mother and longer-term depression of their daughters. Longer-term depression was reported in one-fifth of maternal deaths and in one-quarter of the paternal deaths.

One in five volunteers reported that they were so affected by the death of their parent that they needed a psychiatric referral, there were a slightly higher number of females reporting this than males. Bereaved children have been found to be twice as likely to have a later psychiatric referral than those not so bereaved (Rutter 1966). There was no link in this study between age at the death of the parent and psychiatric referral. However, none of the pre-school volunteers had made such a referral, suggesting that these may have been the least problematic group of all, as well as reinforcing the view that parental death is experienced quite differently for these youngest children than for any other age group.

Vulnerability

One in five volunteers said that they had experienced significant feelings of vulnerability in their subsequent life. One in four of the females reported this, as did one in six of the males. The death of a parent would seem to take away a central pillar in the life of a child, and its removal could remove a large element of the child's trust in life. Having experienced this event some volunteers never seem fully to recover their trust in life again. This can potentially have both a positive and a negative side as described by some volunteers. Fiona, in particular, stands out in Iceberg:

> Fiona, who was attending older secondary school, was determined to 'make the most' of her life after the death of her father, and thought that she should now enjoy it to the full, because she now regarded life as being so very fragile. Fiona described how she 'took life by the horns' and felt that this had been quite a positive element of her experience after the death.

Other volunteers had similar stories about how the death of their parent had quite drastically changed their mind-sets about their enjoyment of life. Their theme, as with Fiona, tended to be along the lines that life is precarious, and we never know when it might end, and therefore we should live it to the full. In a similar vein, another youngster related her story:

Toni said that the experience of the death had made her appreciate 'what she had got', and she did not take things for granted any more. Toni had turned the negative aspect of the death into the positive perception of appreciating life.

Independence

Just over one-seventh of the Iceberg volunteers said that they had now become quite independent in their life after the death of their parent, and that they felt that this was a positive effect. This was mentioned only by volunteers who were in the three oldest age groups and was equally divided between the sexes:

> Jean was a teenager when her father had died, and she spoke how she was initially 'hit very hard' indeed by the death. Jean felt that she had to grow up very quickly, and felt that this had made her a much stronger person in the long run. Jean also said that she realised that things don't last for ever and that she had better get on with her life.

Although some of the older volunteers may have the opportunity to gain greater independence, this may not have always been the case for some of the younger ones. Donna (mentioned earlier) found that she had a loss of independence after the death, as she had to take more of a childcare role. Karen too had a similar experience:

> Karen was a teenager when her mother had died, and she expressed regret as she thought that part of her childhood had been 'stolen'. After the death of her mother, Karen was then expected to take a greater role in helping to bring up her younger siblings.

Confidence

Just over one in ten of the volunteers thought that they had 'no confidence' as a direct result of the experience of their parent's death. All those reporting this loss of confidence were males, being one-third of all the male volunteers. A greater proportion of these related to the death of their mother than to the death of their father. Nearly three-quarters of the males whose mother had died reported this lack of confidence, in contrast to one-fifth where their father had died. This lack of confidence in the males may have related to the loss of their cross-sex role model. Another possibility was that it related in some way to the same-sex relationship they were having with their fathers and perhaps the difficulties and pressures their fathers were under after the death of the volunteers' mothers. In contrast, one of the female volunteers, Eva, said that the parental death had made her stronger in the long run:

> Eva felt that if she could overcome the death of her mother, which she thought that she had, then nothing else could really ever affect her so much again. Eva felt that there could be no worse experience for her than the death of her mother, and that she had coped with and survived that loss, and was stronger for the experience.

Relationship difficulties

One-fifth of the volunteers considered that the insecurity they had felt about life after the death of their parent had filtered through into their own relationships, and relationship separations were often reported. These volunteers thought that their own relationship problems as adults related directly to the effects of the death of their parent. Over one-quarter of the females reported this insecurity as a long-term effect of the death, compared with just over one-tenth of the males. Relationships perhaps do seem to end more frequently today than in previous eras, and a high percentage of marriages break down. This may be for a variety of reasons, for example there is perhaps less stigma now attached to events like divorce. It is very difficult to untangle the effects of the death of the parent from the general cultural climate. However, it was the perception of some volunteers that the effect of the parental death had led to their own relationship difficulties, and therefore that is the reality for these volunteers.

Some volunteers said that they still had difficulties in either talking with relations about the death or even keeping in touch with them, such was the impact of the death:

> Laura said that the family was devastated by the sudden death of her father, but that she still could not talk with her brother about the death, even though it had happened several years before.

> Gordon was 9 years old at the time of the death of his father. Gordon said that he has never since talked with either his mother or his brother about the death. His mother even destroyed all the photographs of his father, and it was as if the man had never existed.

There were many other reports of siblings being unable to communicate with each other about the death of their parent, even in adulthood.

Moving house

One-third of the volunteers eventually moved house as a direct result of the death of their parent. This may well be underreporting, as perhaps the younger children may not have connected a house move in this way with the parental death, and not have reported it as an effect. Moving house may also bring with it a change in area and school, with other potential losses, as described earlier. The reports of moving house were equally divided between maternal and paternal deaths.

Remarriages

One-fifth of the volunteers said that their surviving parents had remarried after the death. There was a greater proportion of remarriages in maternal compared to paternal deaths: 55 per cent of new partners were where the volunteer's mother had died, and 45 per cent where the father had died.

A marriage is the formal introduction into the family of a new partner for the surviving parent. The reports may be an underestimate of the relationships in which their remaining parents were involved, as some may have entered into less formal new relationships that would still, at least to a degree, impact on the volunteers. The volunteers, in some cases, may also not have thought of a new partner for their parent as being a long-term effect of the bereavement.

Economic effects

One-sixth of the volunteers reported experiencing longer-term economic difficulties after the death of their parent. This seems to be a low figure and it may be, especially for the younger volunteers, that they were unaware of the implications or just accepted life as they found it. The surviving parent may also not have made the children aware of their economic difficulties. There was a greater proportion of economic difficulties reported by the volunteers where their father had died; only one-sixth related to the death of a mother. The death of the father therefore seems more likely to bring with it economic difficulties than did the death of the mother. One of the mothers who took part in Iceberg, Alice, took the view that perhaps in most cases the death of a father could bring with it economic catastrophe, although this was not always the case:

> Alice had a young family when her professional husband had died suddenly. Alice thought that the moneys she had obtained from life assurance and from other schemes, together with the help given from her husband's former occupational provision, did much to help to ameliorate these difficulties. Alice was able to keep the family in the same house, and she had adequate money.

Alice's experience may not have been one shared by the majority of widows, but it does show how a death may well have economic implications. Alice's view was that without economic security, she could well have had to sell the family house and move to smaller accommodation, with possibly the children having to move school.

Separation anxiety

One-fifth of the female volunteers said that they experienced long-term separation anxiety, as did one in twenty-five of the males, a significant sex difference. There was also a weak link with age and separation anxiety, as most of the Iceberg volunteers reporting this effect were in the youngest three age groups. This would seem to be intuitively correct, as the older children may well already have achieved a good measure of separation from their parents.

Vulnerability

About 4 per cent of the volunteers, all females, reported being physically abused as a direct result of the death of their parent. Paula, a teenager at the time of her father's death, reported being sexually abused by a family 'friend'. This level of the reports may well have been an underestimate of abuse, as there were further reports of being 'vulnerable' from one-fifth of the volunteers, and by one-quarter of all the females, which may have hinted at abuse or of the perceived potential threat. The volunteers may have been understandably reluctant to fully disclose their experiences.

Loss of role models

One-sixteenth of the volunteers reported the lack of role models as a long-term effect of the death of their parent. These reports were equally divided between the sexes, but were reported only by volunteers in the youngest four age groups. One-third of the females and three-quarters of the males had lost their same-sex role model through the death of their parent. Two-thirds of the females and one-quarter of the males had lost their cross-sex role model. Parents would seem to play an important part of how children gain an idea both of their own identity and role, as well as their schema and expectations of the opposite sex. I did find it surprising that relatively few volunteers raised this aspect as an issue. This may have been a lack of realisation for some of the volunteers, or perhaps it may have been that the older ones had already developed a good concept in the area of role models, or had other alternatives made available. Some volunteers said that things were not always easy at puberty, especially where the same-sex parent had died:

> Val was 10 at the time of her mother's death and told how shortly afterwards she began her periods and felt very em-barrassed having to discuss the subject with her dad, the only adult with whom she felt she could confide.

'Missed out'

One-tenth of the volunteers, all females, felt that they had 'missed out' because of the death of their parent. These volunteers were all in the three oldest age groups and there was no connection between the sex of the parent dying. I had expected the aspect of 'missing out' to be reported at a far higher rate than by just one-tenth of the volunteers. It may have been such an obvious answer for the volunteers that they had really taken it as 'given' response.

Education

Just over one-tenth of the volunteers thought that their education had suffered directly as a result of the death of their parent. There were no sex or age differences to this response. Second or third level elements of losses caused by the trigger of the parental death seemed to be at play here. Some volunteers moved area and school, and felt correctly that this was both unsettling and disruptive. For other volunteers, the death came at a crucial time in relation to their exams, and several commented that their education had been delayed or interrupted by their parent's death. Some volunteers continued their education into their adult life:

> Joyce felt that the death of her father had affected her education for a number of reasons, including the disruption caused by changes in her schools. Joyce found that she developed her education beyond the age of compulsory education through the Open University.

Other volunteers also continued to develop academically through opportunities such as the Open University, and they were rightly proud of their achievements. Some continued to regret that their education had been disrupted and they had not been able to find the opportunity to develop in that area:

Paul felt that he was engaged in quite a menial occupation at work. Paul regretted not achieving what he regarded as his full potential in education, which he connected directly with the death of his parent and the subsequent disruption it caused.

The problems the volunteers reported in their education did not always relate to the disruption caused by moving schools. One-tenth of the volunteers reported that they had truanted over the longer term; one-quarter of the males admitted to playing truant. Most of those who truanted were males, all of whom had experienced the death of their father. Often missing school led to the volunteers being bullied, as they had no 'protective' group of friends. The effect of the bullying just led to the volunteers choosing to truant more – a vicious circle had developed.

The Iceberg volunteers first began to report truancy a year after the death of their parent. Two years after the deaths, there was starting to be a division between two of the subgroups.

About 4 per cent of the volunteers (all males) said that they 'hated school' after the parental death. In contrast the females tended to report that they had no interest in school. Another 4 per cent of the volunteers (all females) actually focused on their academic work at school and became high achievers. A similar number also focused on sporting achievements.

Substance abuse

A minority of the males became involved in substance abuse; as with truancy, all were after the deaths of their fathers. Substance abuse was reported by just under one-tenth of the males although by none of the females. There is the danger of underreporting by the Iceberg volunteers. Cigarette users, for example, are unlikely to describe the substance they use, tobacco, as an abuse, but many would argue that this is the correct description, and the same point could apply to alcohol.

Crime

Two males said that they were involved in crime and 'became hard' after the death of their fathers. There were also reports by some of the mothers involved in the study that some of their children became involved, at least temporarily, in petty crime.

Other effects

There were other minority reports made by some volunteers:

- the loss of religious faith after parental death
- long-term nightmares and flashbacks
- male volunteers reported long-term feelings of bitterness and resentfulness
- females tended to report fear-based reaction while males reported anger type reactions.

Chapter 16

The age at which volunteers gained an idea of death

One focus of Iceberg was to establish when the children first gained the idea of death. Table 16.1 shows the responses that the volunteers gave to this question.

Table 16.1 The age at which the volunteers first gained the idea of death	
Response	%
Pre-school	7
5–7 yr	34
8–11 yr	27
12–15 yr	9
16+ yr	3
No recall	20

Although some volunteers said that they did not gain an idea of death until they were teenagers, one in fourteen said that they did so at 4 years old. It has been contended that most children gain an adult understanding of death by the age of 12 (Zach 1978). This does tie in with the Piagetian notion of children achieving the capability of abstract thought at around 12 years (Lovell 1973). Table 16.2 shows the answers given by the volunteers as to the age when they first gained the idea of death.

Table 16.2 The percentage of children, by age, when first gaining the idea of death					
Age	Pre-school	5–7 yr	8–11 yr	12–15 yr	16+ yr
Percentage	9	43	34	11	3
Cumulative	9	52	86	97	100

Table 16.2 tends to support the idea that by 12 years old most children have gained a good idea of death. Over three-quarters of the volunteers considered that they had gained an idea of death by the age of 12. There were still some puzzling reports, for example it did seem strange that some as old as 16 years said that they had only just gained their first idea of death. Some volunteers, whose parents had died when they were in the older age groups, did comment that they did not appreciate the effects of death, and the impact that it potentially would have on their life. Others related how they had only really understood death when their parent had died. Just under one-tenth of the volunteers were of pre-school age when their parent died, although none of this group reported gaining an understanding of death until they were of junior age. Ben was a pre-schooler at the time of his father's death:

> Ben said that he only really gained an idea of death at the age of 9, when his uncle had died. This was despite Ben having experienced the death of his father at a much younger age.

Even Iceberg volunteers who were slightly older than Ben made similar reports:

Adam said that although, at 5 years of age, he knew what death was in a sort of abstract way, it was only when his own father died five years later, that Adam felt that he gained a much fuller and real understanding of the concept.

Sean was 5 when he first encountered 'death' and he kept looking in the sky for his grandparents, wondering on which cloud they lived.

There seemed to be two things happening with the reports being made by volunteers. Some volunteers seemed to have answered this question in terms of their first experience of death, and the realisation that things do not go on forever. This was such as when a pet had died:

Kylie said that she bred mice when she was a child, and that she was well aware that living things died, even at the young age of 4 years.

Katie told how she gained her first idea of death at around the age of 5 when she found her pet budgie dead in its cage. Before then her pets had just mysteriously disappeared without any mention.

In contrast, other volunteers seemed to have answered this question directly in relation to their parental bereavement experience. It seems very unlikely that a 12-year-old child will not have at least some notion of death, especially bearing in mind the remarks made by Kylie. It seems that for at least some volunteers, they had gained the idea of the impact of death only by going through the experience of having a parent die. To claim that children gain an understanding of death at a particular age seems to be too simplistic and begs the question of what 'understanding' death actually means. Children learn through interacting with their environment and context, although this may of course be either limited or else extended by their cognitive abilities and their life experiences. A 4-year-old child will only understand death in the terms of the experience, maturity and understanding of a 4 year old. This was the case with some volunteers in the younger aged groups, who related their experiences of bereavement around the change of their care providers at the time after the death of their parent. For the older volunteers the experience was different, as, for example, they were forced into roles that were neither anticipated nor often not welcomed, such as the care of their younger siblings or of their father.

The dying patients in the Kubler-Ross (1982) study and the widows in the Parkes (1986) studies, both referred to earlier, were mature and old in comparison to the Iceberg volunteers, who were children at the time their parent died. Those dying patients and widows would have had far wider life experiences, expectations and understandings than would the Iceberg volunteers as children. The older adults would have been able to predict future losses leading from a death, which the volunteers, as children, could not have been expected to be able to have contemplated. Many future expectations are likely to be beyond the conceptual understanding of young children, and if these are not realised then they cannot be mourned for in the same way as an older person. The older adults, having experienced more of life, would have developed expectations about their own future life, and surely would have more of a 'future loss' component in their grieving than would the younger children. A mature individual, having gone through the experience of having children, could appreciate and mourn future losses for themselves if they died, such as not actually seeing their own children growing up and their own grandchildren. In comparison, the grieving of the younger children would seem to revolve more around the change of the carer and as such be more fixed in the 'here and now' of life. For the younger children in Iceberg the future would be only just a short time ahead.

Some volunteers in the older age group said that they gained their first understanding of death at the age when their parent actually died. This seems to have been because they had not realised the full impact that death can have until it actually happened within their experience. Death for them was not just the loss of a parent, the realisation that their parent was actually dead and would not return, nor was it just the loss of a carer. The death of the parent brought with it other potential difficulties, such as the isolation felt both at school and at home. There were also further secondary losses, which flowed directly from the death of their parent:

- moving home
- changing school
- economic problems
- partners for the surviving parents.

For many of the Iceberg volunteers, their lives were changed dramatically and irrevocably, moving to a trajectory previously neither predicted nor for many welcomed, well beyond the effect of the loss of their parent as an individual person. Table 16.3 shows the average age of the Iceberg volunteers reporting when they first gained the idea of death. The mean scores for each of the Iceberg age groups are shown in Table 16.3.

Table 16.3 The average ages when the volunteers first gained the idea of death							
	Pre-school	5–7 yr	8–11 yr	12–15 yr	16+ yr	Mean	Mean 2
Age in years	9	5.6	8.2	8.4	9.2	8.2	8.5

The overall mean age when the Iceberg volunteers said that they first gained the idea of death was 8.2 years. The 'mean 2' figure in Table 16.3 is the mean age when the data from the volunteers of the infant aged group are removed from the total data pool. The volunteers in the pre-school group reported gaining an understanding of death at the age of 9 years old, the second highest of the averages of all the age groups. This seemed to be counter-intuitive, as the pre-school children were the group having experienced the death of a parent at the youngest age! The volunteers in this age group reported that they had not really understood or grasped the full reality of death until they had actually experienced another close bereavement later in their life:

> Alison was 4 years old at the time of her dad's death, and she said that while she knew that he had 'gone', she had no real understanding of the implications of the death at the time it took place. This realisation came only when she was older.

This reinforces the suggestion that the experiences of the pre-school group contained issues more around separation and change of carer than they did around a conceptual understanding of death.

Table 16.3 shows that the mean age of the Iceberg volunteers reporting gaining an understanding of death was quite similar for all of the age groups except those in the infant age group. The pattern is different for these volunteers having experienced the death of a parent when they were of infant age, as they reported gaining an understanding at the age of 6, this being the age which they actually had experienced the death of their parent. It seems that this group of volunteers experienced the death of their parent in a different way from their pre-school peers. While the pre-school group seemed not to have gained a full grasp of the implications of the death, and for them the experience was more an issue of attachment and separation, this was not the case for the infant age group. The infant age group may have been an appropriate age to have a greater cognitive understanding of death as a concept, which was then 'overlaid' with their actual experience of the death of their parent. This may have enabled them to grasp the experience at a greater cognitive level than their pre-school peers.

The average scores reported by the volunteers in terms of reporting their understanding death were all within 0.7 of a year of the mean, whereas the infant age group average score was 2.9 years away from the mean. This could suggest that volunteers in the junior and secondary age groups actually had some grasp of the idea of death before the death of their parent, which seems a reasonable proposition.

Chapter 17

Different types of loss

It became apparent during the project that the Iceberg volunteers had experienced quite complex losses after the death of their parent. To describe the experience of the volunteers after the death of their parent as bereavement was far too simplistic. There is no generic template for loss that can be equally applied to all children, as their experiences are all individual and unique. It was possible to identify some of the patterns and themes of children's losses after a parental death and these are shown in Table 17.1.

Table 17.1 Different types of loss encountered by children		
A	Attachment	An appreciation of the separation from a carer
B	Bereavement	The appreciation of the death of the individual and the immediate implications
C	Collateral	Second and third level losses that flow directly as effects from the death
D	Delayed	Losses relating to the death of the individual that become evident only later
E	Expectations	The anticipation of future losses relating to the death of the individual

Type A loss

The Iceberg volunteers in the pre-school group seemed to experience the death of their parent in a quite different way from the other groups in the project. Their loss seemed to be more associated with issues of attachment, shown as 'A loss' in Table 17.1. These volunteers, at the time of the death of their parent, did not really seem to mourn the parent's death in the sense of the parent being an individual, but rather more in the role of their carer. It was only later in their life, around the age of 9, that the fuller impact of the death became apparent to the pre-schooler, and the implications of what had happened became clearer. This particular group had relatively little recall of the events at the time of the parental death, and they even lacked clear memories of their parent.

Type B loss

The second strand, 'B loss', as shown in Table 17.1, is the more traditional type of bereavement response reported by the Iceberg volunteers and relates directly to the death of their parent as an individual person. The volunteers were grieving the death of an individual with whom they had a more personal relationship, this beyond them just being their carer. This loss was still within the limitations of the individual's cognitive level and also their life experiences at the time of the death. Only Iceberg volunteers in the four oldest age groups reported 'B loss'. These volunteers did seem both to mourn and miss their parent on a more personal level than did their pre-school peers, and memories of their parents were often etched in their minds. These volunteers, as children, did have an appreciation that their parent was actually dead, and that they would not return, something not really experienced by the youngest children. This level of understanding was epitomised by the reports of the infant group as to their understanding of death, as described in the previous section. The infant age group also had the lowest score in terms of the age at which they thought that they gained an understanding of death, coinciding with the age at which they had actually experienced parental death.

'B loss' also seemed to be dependent on the developmental stage of the volunteers when they were children. For some volunteers it was the realisation that their parent will no longer be available and able to take them out on trips or for treats. In a sense this was egocentric and based on self-interest, although other volunteers still did show signs of quite sophisticated responses to the death, as previously mentioned, such as the relief that their parent was no longer suffering after having endured a long terminal illness. The level of 'B loss' seemed to increase with age and maturity, and is another reason why it is difficult to accept that there is a generic template for grieving that can be equally applied to all children.

It may be that some volunteers in the youngest age group actually experienced this 'B loss' later in their lives, when they realised the significance of the death of their parent. The relationship the Iceberg volunteers had with their parent, at the pre-school age, seems to have been qualitatively different from those who were older at the time of their parent's death. In later years, the younger children seem to have caught up and also 'mourned' the loss of their parent in terms beyond that of the parent's role, but they seemed to have had no real memories on which to attach what could be described as true mourning for a specific individual person. Perhaps their grieving was later in a more abstract way, even perhaps more idealistic, although this was not really revealed in the study. The younger children all seemed to have experienced 'A loss', with the older ones additionally experiencing 'B loss'.

Both types were associated with the immediate loss of either a carer or of a parent, and perhaps needed time for 'resolution', using a term from traditional loss models. The outcome for both the 'A' and 'B' losses seemed also to depend on within-child factors, as well as on the context of the death. Some volunteers achieved what they considered to be 'normality' within a relatively short time after the death of their parent, at least in comparison to the received wisdom regarding resolution. This was also despite what can only be described as a general lack of adult facilitation for the volunteers, who generally considered themselves quite isolated and found teachers and other adults in their life to be quite difficult to approach.

Type C loss

The third type of loss shown in Table 17.1 is 'C loss', the collateral loss flowing directly from the death of the parent, but not actually related to the parent as a carer or individual person. Before the death of their parent the volunteers were on a particular life trajectory. The death often led to things irrevocably changing for the volunteers, although this was not necessarily always for the worse in the long term. 'C loss' was dependent upon how the circumstances developed after the death of their parent. For some volunteers their lives were thrown into turmoil, and they were involved in yet more second and third level losses after the death of their parent. These changes were losses caused by life adjustments after the death of their parent, rather than by the grief reactions relating to the death. These collateral losses included some volunteers having to move home, in some cases there were complete moves of area, sometimes very quickly after the death of their parent. These volunteers then had to contend with yet further changes and losses, such as moving from their school and from their friends and teachers whom they knew. Many volunteers reported either 'A' or 'B' losses, or even both, and these additional and often not insignificant changes of 'C loss' were therefore overlaid on the 'A' and 'B' losses, such as in the case of Daniel.

Daniel was 8 years old at the time of his dad's death, and he was suddenly 'taken away' by his mum to a new life in an area far away from his home and to live with relatives he had hardly ever seen before. This was a total culture shock for Daniel, and he needed to develop new relationships, not only with his relatives, but also with new friends as well as with new teachers, all of whom who spoke with different accents from his. Daniel described feeling that he was a refugee.

Emily's story has already been told, how she had experienced not only moving area away from her school and friends, but also the destruction of her pets. Emily's experience was another example as to how losses unconnected with grieving for the parent can arise after their death. Many volunteers said that they moved home after their parent had died, some had also experienced their parent's remarrying and others experienced economic difficulties at home. These further losses included the introduction of a step-parent into the family home, with the attention of the surviving parent now being at least marginally diverted. Some volunteers, especially females, now had to fit into unwelcome roles, such as carrying out babysitting duties, cooking, and looking after their family. Some of the volunteers in the older age group left home quite quickly to escape such situations. There were also both reports and hints of abuse made by some females. Richard, whose story has already been told, said that, after his father's death, his mum went out to work, and that things at home were never the same again. The halving of the parental 'caring team' and the loss of role models also seemed to have led to difficulty for some volunteers, sometimes related to the reports of substance abuse and truancy.

Collateral losses were sometimes economic as well as organisational, relating to the family network. Insurance cover enabled some of the families to remain in the family house after the death of the father, thereby keeping an element of stability for the children. Collateral loss will depend on the context and the individual circumstances after the death of a parent.

Type D loss

The fourth type of loss identified in Iceberg was that of delayed or 'D loss', shown in Table 17.1. 'D loss' is grief for the person who has died, and not collateral loss, but grieving which could not have been anticipated by the children at the time of their parent's death. 'D loss' relates to the cognitive level of the Iceberg volunteers as well as to their life experiences. There seems to be a general consensus that by 12 years old, most children will have gained an adult understanding of death. This was also confirmed by the Iceberg research. However, this conclusion seems too simplistic. The experience of a 12-year-old youngster must be qualitatively different from that of a 20-year-old adult, as it would be from a 30 or 40 year old. As individuals grow older and have more experience of life, so their individual experience of death must surely also be different.

The 'D loss' lies in wait for either the child or adult, and it comes into play only at the appropriate time when they are in a position that they are able to appreciate it. It is 'B loss' moving forward and developing through the life experience which is gained only over time, and becomes more sophisticated. An 8-year-old child is unlikely to mourn the loss of their dead parent not ever seeing their grandchildren. That particular loss would not seem to be apparent at the age of 12 years, and perhaps not even at the age of 20 years:

Nora was 7 at the time of her mother's death. Nora told how much later in her life she was in a maternity ward after having given birth to her own child and was then visited by her husband. The occasion was, of course, joyful, but at the same time Nora felt tinges of sadness when seeing the other women in the ward being visited by their mothers. It was only then that Nora realised another implication relating to the death of her mother.

That particular loss, that Nora's own mother would never see her grandchildren, had been waiting for both the context and an awareness to appear before becoming apparent to Nora. Many volunteers also felt that they realised the fuller implications of the death of their parent, not at the time, but only at a much later date.

This was also the case with the pre-schooler volunteers, who reported gaining an understanding of death some years after their parent had died. These younger children experienced 'A loss' at the time of their parent's death, but not 'B loss'. They later experienced 'D loss' when their awareness and life experiences were such as to enable them to actually appreciate what they actually had lost at the time. 'B loss' is actually experienced at the time of the death, the grief for an individual who had died; 'D loss', in contrast, is that loss which can be mourned for only at the time when there is a realisation that there has been a loss.

Type E loss

The fifth type of loss reported by the Iceberg volunteers is 'E loss', as shown in Table 17.1, and is grief for the loss of a future event. 'E loss' again relates to the cognitive and life experiences of the individual. 'E loss' is similar to 'B loss', in that it is grief relating to the individual person, but it is that part of grief relating to events which have not yet happened. This contrasts with events that have already taken place, memories, or those predictable by the individual at the time of the death. To experience 'E loss', the individual needs to be able to predict and project their loss into the future. The young child who has had the experience of a parent dying will realise that their parent can no longer take them out on trips and buy them ice-cream. The youngsters will be unlikely to realise the implications relating to their later life, for example that their parent will not see them pass milestones such as graduation from college or see their own children, the dead parent's grandchildren. Sheila's father died in her teens, and she was now in her early twenties:

> Sheila told how she felt pangs of grief when her father did not attend her graduation, and realises that he will also not attend her wedding.

Adults may well experience all these types of losses after the death of a loved one as they have both the life experience and cognitive awareness to be able to project and predict these future losses realistically. 'E loss' is close to 'D loss', but is apparent before the event takes place, rather than when it takes place. Nora experienced 'D loss' in the maternity hospital when she saw other mothers with both their parents. If Nora had realised this before the event then it would have been an expected future loss or 'E loss'.

Different types of loss

The Iceberg volunteers had experienced a variety of discrete and separate losses. An awareness that there are individual factors within a bereavement after a death is important in terms of both interventions to help and an awareness of the potential implications for children after the death of a parent. These should be helpful for parents, relations, professionals and others who encounter children who have experienced the death of a parent.

Chapter 18

The experience of death by the Iceberg volunteers

The experience of death by Iceberg volunteers compared with adults

The experiences of the volunteers as children was quite different from the adult experience in several ways: adults tend to have more control and power over circumstances than do children. This relates both to the children's understanding of what is happening at the time of the death, and also to their involvement in the rituals after the death of their parent. Adults are far more likely to have accurate information about what is happening at a time of crisis. Children may lack the very basic information about what is happening, and may not know where to obtain information, assuming that they even know what questions to ask. The volunteers were frequently left in the dark and were not aware what was happening. This lack of awareness leads to the potential for fantasies of things being far worse than the reality. Adults have control over the rituals after a death, such as the chapel of rest and the funeral. Many volunteers were excluded from these rituals through the power of adults. Adults are also far more likely to have control in terms of the collateral losses flowing from the death. Adults will be deciding whether or not to move house and in the medium term they will choose whether or not to enter into relationships that may directly or indirectly impact on their children.

Children may not have their grieving facilitated by the adults around them. Some volunteers would not have welcomed this facilitation; although a minority seemed to survive the experience of the death of their parent with resilience, for others there were long-term difficulties. Although the focus of Iceberg was on bereavement by the death of a parent, the differences between adults and children potentially spans all the other losses in life, such as those of parental separation, moving house, or the transition between phases of education. Here children may also lack both information and control over events.

Adults will probably experience all the different facets of loss in one fell swoop of intensity, or at least over a relatively short period of time. Children may not have this sort of experience, and they may gradually accumulate losses 'A' to 'E' over a much longer period of time. This may explain why such a large proportion had difficulties beyond the traditional two year period of grieving, as well as why many others said that they were feeling 'normal' relatively soon after the death of their parent.

Information and control

Many of the Iceberg volunteers related how they did not understand what was happening at the time of the death. Children, like adults, find the initial news of the death of their parent quite difficult to absorb. This is not really a surprise, since the death of a parent, a key figure in the life of the child, strikes at the heart of the 'given world' for the young person, as a major given assumption in their life is suddenly removed. Children are often quite isolated both at home and at school by this experience, one way in which the experience of death for children may differ from that of many adults. Adults potentially have other avenues of support available, such as counselling or seeking help from their general practitioner, routes perhaps not so easily available to children.

Children should not be overlooked after a death; they do need to have clear information about what is happening, in terms they can understand. Without adequate information, children will potentially be left with fantasies which may well far exceed the reality of the situation. Information needs to be given to youngsters in terms of their cognitive and experiential levels. Providing complex technical information to children may only serve to confuse. As noted in Chapter 4, they may not understand how a heart is 'attacked', or how something as gentle as a 'stroke' can kill you. There is an issue of effective communication. Some female volunteers reported that they initially had fear reactions on hearing the news of the death of their parent, and some male volunteers reported anger. These potential responses need to be borne in mind when telling children. Careful consideration could be given to decisions that are taken by adults in the post death period, and the potential effects these choices may have on the bereaved children. Many volunteers found that lack of control in the situation was an issue, and involving children as far as is possible in decisions could be one way to help to minimise these difficulties.

Factors relating to more positive outcomes for children

There were some wide variations in the experiences of the Iceberg volunteers. Some encountered few difficulties during the initial months after the death of their parent, while others reported experiencing problems for years after the death. The volunteers had been asked explicitly how their school either helped or hindered them after the death of their parent and also how their school could have helped them more. The

Iceberg data were analysed with a focus on those volunteers who reported high scores in terms of how their school helped, to look for common features within this positive outcome subgroup.

Half of the subgroup were male volunteers, which suggested that there may be better outcomes for many males, as they were in the minority as Iceberg volunteers, although the differences were not significant in the statistical sense. Males tended to report reaching a state of normality far quicker than did the females, although the latter did catch up and overtake in the medium term. The female volunteers also reported far more difficulties around the general area of depression in the longer term.

The subgroup contained more parents who had died suddenly. The context of the death of the parent was considered as a possible factor. Perhaps those volunteers whose parent's death was anticipated had better outcomes than where the death had been sudden and unexpected. If the death had been anticipated, volunteers may have had time to say goodbye to their parent, and also to come to terms with the death before it actually happened. However, the Iceberg volunteers would not really have known what to expect when their parent actually died, and knowing in advance that their parent was dying may not have been helpful. Three-quarters of the 'positive' group had the experience of a sudden death, compared to half in the Iceberg group as a whole. This seems counter-intuitive, although it may be that children experiencing the dying of their parent over a long period suffer a continued series of stress and loss experiences. These children may in a sense have had to grieve both for the suffering of their parent during the time before the death, as well as grieving for the forthcoming death itself, these in effect being 'E' losses. This may further complicate the experience of the volunteers and have made it even harder for them to resolve their loss.

The subgroup contained more paternal deaths: one-fifth of the volunteers in the positive group experienced the death of their mother, compared to one-third in the total Iceberg group. This suggests that the outcomes tended to be more problematic in the case of a maternal compared to a paternal death. Again this difference between the 'positive' group and the whole subject pool was not statistically significant.

There were no significant differences between the 'positive' subgroup in outcomes between whether the Iceberg volunteers had visited their parent at the chapel of rest or not; although the reports of the volunteers who attended the rituals were in the main very positive. There were more negative outcomes for those volunteers who had been forbidden to attend the rituals or else distracted. One factor did seem to be whether the volunteers had been offered a choice of being involved in the rituals.

> Barbara was a teenager at the time of the sudden death of her father, and she chose not to attend either the chapel of rest or the funeral. Barbara was in the more positive outcome group. Barbara said that what was important for her was that she had been given the choice and therefore had an element of control over events.

Some of the other factors in the 'positive' group related to school and the social support from peers, as well as to an apparent resilience within the particular volunteers. The subgroup contained more who found their teachers easier to approach. One-fifth of the volunteers in the 'positive' group said that they found their teachers easy to approach and talk with, as opposed to just one-sixteenth in the Iceberg group as a whole. Giles in the 'positive' group was an example of this:

Giles was a teenager at the time of the death of his mother and he told how he felt that adults were quite easy to approach. This meant that Giles felt that he always potentially had somebody to talk things through about the death, if he so needed.

One-third of the volunteers in the 'positive' group had easy access to adult support, over twice the rate of the Iceberg volunteers in general. This perhaps led to an easier facilitation of these volunteers' grief. The majority of the 'positive' group seemed to gain some support either from adults or from their peers: 40 per cent of the 'positive' subgroup thought that their peers at school had helped them just through having somebody with whom they could talk.

Some of the Iceberg volunteers did seem to be particularly resilient. Chris and Viv were two examples of Iceberg volunteers who seemed to take the initiative in their life:

Chris was 11 years old at the time of the death of his mother and he said that he thought that the adults around him seemed to be quite useless, rather like 'headless chickens'. Chris said how one day, shortly after the death, he just thought 'stuff them all' and decided that he would fend for himself from then on.

Chris's relatively good outcome seems to relate to his taking control, at least psychologically, at a time when everything around him seemed to be going out of control.

Viv was a teenager at the sudden death of her father and said how she initially felt very insecure. That phase did not last for long for Viv, and she was then determined to make herself a good life.

Viv, in a similar way to Chris, had seized control of her life. The modal age of the 'positive' subgroup was 12, close to the modal age of the main subject pool of 11 years, suggesting that the age of the volunteer was not an issue in terms of them being in the more 'positive' outcome subgroup. There seemed to be no other factors relating to a more positive outcome after the death of the volunteer's parent.

Chapter 19

Conclusions to the research questions

The project investigated four research questions. These are now briefly revisited.

1. *What is the experience of parental death like for children, in terms of their grieving, power, and the support, facilitation or otherwise they receive from their family and school?*

It was often assumed that children pass through quite similar experiences to adults after the death of a significant person in their life, such as a parent. The results from Iceberg suggest that the experience of loss can be quite different for children, even if they do seem to have an adult understanding of death. The experiences of pre-schoolers as a group seemed qualitatively different from other children. Their loss seemed to relate to that of the carer and separation. These younger children gained an understanding of death only in later life, often when bereavement occurred after the age when they were able to have a greater cognitive understanding. It may be that mourning and the stages of grieving are set against the general backdrop of other factors, such as the age of the child and the context of the death. Many volunteers taking part in Iceberg experienced collateral losses caused indirectly through the death of their parent, but not directly related to bereavement. These further losses included major life changes, such as moving house, or having their parent remarry, and were overlaid onto the context of the death of their parent. While adults may also experience these consequential losses, the children seemed more helpless and to lack control over events.

The volunteers in Iceberg seemed to divide into two broad groups. The first group recovered from the death of the parent relatively quickly, well before the traditional two year grieving period. For other Iceberg volunteers, their difficulties extended far beyond the two year mourning, and well into later adult life. Powerlessness was a major issue for many of the Iceberg volunteers. They tended to report that they did not really understand what was happening at the time of the death of their parent. A paradox was that they found teachers at their school and other adults difficult to approach, and it was these adults who were the potential source of the information they were craving. None of the volunteers reported having shared discussions with their surviving parent on major events, such as moving house or a remarriage. While these issues are such that perhaps children ought not to be highly involved, the whole experience for them tended to be one of powerlessness. The typical experience was that children were only told what was happening to them at very short notice.

At the time of a death, things are likely to be in crisis, and children may not understand what is happening, partly through the lack of information. The surviving parent may be at the hospital or otherwise engaged, and carers may not want to provide this information. It is perhaps only slowly, if at all, that children are told the whole reality of what has and what is happening. This could be because the parent is preoccupied, or perhaps their motive is to protect the child. In either case, there are implications for successful grieving, and for the future trust of children, if they are not kept as informed by the parent as their understanding allows. The first task of grieving is accepting the reality of the loss, and this may well be delayed for children (Worden 1984). Children do generally seem to find things out later, perhaps from their peers, and in the school playground. What they glean may not only be incorrect or misleading but also may lead them to lose trust in the adults close to them. The Iceberg volunteers generally did not find either their teachers or other adults easy to approach and talk with about the death, and hence generally they did not receive adult facilitation.

2. How can adults, in particular teachers, give effective support for bereaved children at school, what helps and what hinders the grieving process?

Adults tended not to facilitate the grief of the Iceberg volunteers, either at home or at school. Some volunteers said that their school had helped them by omission, the staff at school not attempting to engage with them around the death of their parent. These volunteers actually welcomed being left alone, although it does not seem to have been a planned intervention by the school. Those volunteers were asked how things could have been made better for them at school. They provided a series of suggestions, many quite lightweight interventions, such as having somebody to listen to them, or an acknowledgement of their loss. The Iceberg volunteers all too frequently seemed to encounter a wall of silence at their school. This may have been because the teachers just did not know what to say, or because they did not want to risk upsetting the children. There may have been issues around teachers and their own losses, or they may not see it as their role to become involved in so supporting bereaved children. In some cases, children welcomed being left alone, but this was not the case for many others who experienced a sense of isolation and of being ignored on their return.

Some volunteers suggested that counselling at their school would have helped them, this being a much heavier intervention. Many volunteers thought that loss education in the curriculum and training for teachers would also have helped them during their bereavement. The strategies mentioned by the volunteers were potentially the first-aid that did not take place at the time of their parental death. It is only possible to speculate, but the longer-term difficulties reported by some of the volunteers may have been avoided had an intervention taken place at the time of the death.

3.   Is the issue of loss and bereavement addressed by schools, and if so is it done in a meaningful way, and does it have positive outcomes in terms of helping children?

Research in the context of Humberside schools suggested that loss and bereavement were generally not addressed in schools, although there was some interesting but uncoordinated work taking place in some of the schools in the study (Holland 1993, Holland and Ludford 1995). These results were also based on the perceptions of teachers rather than the children. Only one of the volunteers in Iceberg said that they had any loss education at their school. It may be that schools had actually delivered loss education, but that this had not been so grasped by children. In any event, if delivered it does not seem to have been effective, as the Iceberg volunteers as a group said that their schools had done little to help them to prepare for the death of their parent. Another explanation may be that with the five year time embargo on interviewing, this underestimates the amount of work that is taking place currently in schools.

4. How does the experience of bereavement affect children in the short, medium and long term? Are they more likely to have time off school, through illness, as an indirect effect of unresolved grief?

The results of Iceberg showed wide variations in the longer-term experience of the volunteers who took part. A minority of the volunteers achieved a self-described 'normality' relatively quickly after the death. These individuals seemed to be quite resilient and did not appear to suffer long-term effects after the death of their parent. However, for a large number of the volunteers this was not the case. Many considered that their subsequent problems in later life related to their early childhood experience of a parent dying. These difficulties included long-term depression, especially for the female volunteers, and relationship difficulties with their own partners and spouses. Frequently a direct cause was postulated between childhood bereavement and these later problems in life. There was again a mixture of experiences in relation to time off school for reasons such as illness. Some of the Iceberg volunteers did have more time off school, and psychosomatic illnesses were reported, although a minority actually had less time off school. The reasons for this may have related to the new circumstances of the remaining parent and to organisational problems.

Looking for patterns

Some models of grieving tend to suggest that there is a pattern through which individuals pass, much as a train passes along a track. The Iceberg data suggest that to find a single pattern for all bereaved children would be to oversimplify a complex situation. Each child is unique, and there are wide variations of both 'within-child' and also contextual factors influencing the course and outcome of the bereavement. We have difficulty in gaining an insight into each other's experiences (Huxley 1977). Words can be uttered but they can fail to enlighten, and they are really symbols belonging to mutually exclusive realms of experience. I heard or read the perceptions of the Iceberg volunteers, translating them within my own perceptions and experiences, with the danger of distortions. Within this caveat of communication, there were patterns within the data, and the results of the reflections and experiences of the Iceberg volunteers could well help contemporary bereaved children. Schools and teachers can play a key role in both loss education and also in supporting the bereaved young person in school. Adults perhaps need to understand that children's comprehension of death is gradually acquired over time, and that they possibly have a greater actual understanding than is apparent. However, this understanding of death has to be balanced against the limited life experiences of the children, and the true significance and implications of death may be realised only over time and only much later in life. Teachers too need to understand that children will be affected by bereavement in a variety of ways and intensities. Children may need support to resolve the various issues with which they are confronted. They may lack an understanding of what is happening in terms of facts, and also in terms of control. Things just seem 'to happen' to bereaved children, they are in a sense disenfranchised of choice. They may find themselves suddenly uprooted from their home and moving some distance away from their friends, school and neighbourhood, or have the experience of the quick remarriage of their parent. Children's attainment at school may also be affected in their learning and also their behaviour. For some children this may be an increase or a surge in their attainments, academic or sporting, but for others their attainments may decline, especially in the short term. This is hardly surprising, as bereaved children will at times be preoccupied with inner thoughts, and they may well find attention and concentration difficult. Children's response to their lack of control and feelings of exclusion, as well as to the death, may be one of anger and in this way result in adverse behaviour. Other children may be drawn into areas that perhaps they may not have encountered but for the death of their parent. For example, some may play truant, while others may become involved in substance abuse and other activities regarded as being on the fringes of society. Some may be affected by a decline in self-esteem, experiencing a vulnerability that could be reflected in them becoming victims of abuse. All these represent potential outcomes relating to the death of their parent, and teachers can help through an empathetic and sympathetic approach. The Iceberg volunteers reported that they gained much from a simple acknowledgement of their loss, such as a teacher mentioning to them that they were sorry about the death. Others felt that they would have benefited from somebody available just to listen to them, and provide a friendly ear. There seems little to be lost and much to be potentially gained by making a human approach to a bereaved child.

Interview sheet: pupil

Subject number _____

Subject age ____   Subject sex _____

Years since bereavement ____

Age at bereavement ____   Who died _____

Questions

1. 'When your _____ died, what were your first reactions?'

2. 'Did you understand what was happening at the time of the death. If not, what was not clear?'

3. 'Did you visit the chapel of rest and go to the funeral?'

4. 'How did you feel about that?'

5.   'How did you feel when you went back to school?'

6.   'How did school help?'

7.   'Were teachers easy to approach to talk about things?'

8.   'Who did you talk with, if anybody, about the death?'

9.   'Do you feel that schools helped you prepare for the bereavement?'

10. 'Did you have any "loss" or "death" education at school?'

11. 'In what ways did school help/hinder you with bereaving?'

12. 'In what ways do you think that school could have helped more?'

13. 'Did the other adults around help, were they easy to talk to?'

14. 'How did you feel generally about things a month after the death?'

15. 'How did you feel generally about things six months after the death?'

16. 'How did you feel generally about things a year after the death?'

17. 'How did you feel generally about things two years after the death?'

18. 'Did you have more, or less, time off school after the bereavement?'

19. 'Do you think that there have been any medium or long-term effects from the death?'

20. 'Rate on a scale from 0 to 10 (0 low / 10 high) as a general indicator of how school helped you during the bereavement.'

21. 'Rate on a scale from 0 to 10 (0 very isolated / 10 not at all isolated) how isolated you felt in the period up to around a year after the death.'

22. 'Can you remember at about what age you first gained the idea of death?'

23. 'Do you feel that you need support in this area, if so can I help?'

Interview sheet: parent

Subject number _____

Subject age ____   Subject sex _____

Years since bereavement ____

Age of pupil at bereavement ____

Sex of pupil _____   Who died _____

Questions

1. 'Tell me how _____ was after the death.'

2. 'When did _____ return to school after the death?'

3. 'What was _____ like on returning to school?'

4. 'How did school respond to _____'s return to school?'

5. 'After the death did _____ have much time off
    school with illness, was this more or less than
    before?'

6. 'How was _____ a month after the death?'

7. 'How was _____ six months after the death?'

8. 'How was _____ a year after the death?'

9. 'How was _____ two years after the death?'

10. 'Rate on a scale from 0 to 10 (0 low / 10 high) as
    a general indicator of how you consider that
    school helped _____ during the bereavement.'

11. 'What do you think _____ understood about
    death at the time?'

12. 'Do you think that schools can help pupils by dealing with death in the curriculum, such as through PSE [personal and social education]? If so, how?'

13. 'Do you feel that you need support in this area, if so can I help?'

14. Close down, discussions of matters close to the reality of the immediate situation.

References

Books

Abrams, R. (1993) 'Helping teenagers and young adults cope with the death of a parent.' *Bereavement Care 12*, 2,16–18.

Alder, J. (1994) 'Kids growing up scared.' *Newsweek*, January, 43–50.

Archer, J. (1999) *The Nature of Grief.* London: Routledge.

Ariès, P. (1983) *The Hour of our Death.* Aylesbury: Peregrine.

Balk, D. (1983) 'Effects of sibling death on teenagers.' *Journal of School Health 53*, 14–18.

Bannister, P., Burman, E., Parker, I., Taylor, M. and Tindall, C. (1994) *Qualitative Methods in Psychology.* Buckingham: Open University Press.

Barnsley, N. (1995) *Dancing on the Grave, Encounters with Death.* London: John Murray.

Bartlett, F. C. (1932) *Remembering.* Cambridge: Cambridge University Press.

Birtchnell, T. (1970) 'Early parent death and mental illness.' *British Journal of Psychiatry 116*, 281–288.

Birtchnell, T. (1975) 'Psychiatric breakdown following recent parent death.' *British Journal of Medical Psychology 48*, 379–390.

Blackburn, M. (1991) 'Bereaved children and their teachers.' *Bereavement Care 10*, 2, 19–21.

Bowlby, J. (1963) 'Pathological mourning and childhood mourning.' *Journal of the American Psychoanalytical Association 11*, 500.

Bowlby, J. (1973) *Attachment and Loss, Volume 2: Separation.* London: Hogarth.

Branwhite, T. (1994) 'Bullying and student distress: beneath the tip of the iceberg.' *Educational Psychology 14*, 1, 59–71.

Brown, G. W., Harris, T. and Copeland, J. R. (1977) 'Depression and loss.' *British Journal of Psychiatry 130*, 1–18.

Brown, R. and Kulick, J. (1982) 'Flashbulb memory.' In U. Neisser (ed) *Memory Observed.* London: W. H. Freeman.

Bunch, J., Barraclough, B., Nelson, B. and Sainsbury, P. (1971) 'Suicide following the death of a parent.' *Social Psychiatry 6*, 193–199.

Cannell, C. F. and Kahn, R. L. (1968) 'Interviewing.' In G. Lindzey and A. Aronson (eds) *The Handbook of Social Psychology, Volume 2: Research Methods*. New York: Addison Wesley.

Cannon, W. B. (1929) *Bodily Changes in Pain, Hunger, Fear and Rage*. London: Appleton.

Capewell, E. C. (1994) 'Responding to children in trauma: a systems approach for schools.' *Bereavement Care 13*, 1, 2–7.

Central Statistical Office (CSO) (1989) *Social Trends*. London: HMSO.

Chamberlain, M. and Richardson, R. (1983) 'Life and death.' *Oral History Journal 11*, 1, 31–43.

Charlton, T. and Hoye, J. (1987) *The Caring Role of the Primary School*. London: Macmillan.

Cohen, L. and Manion, L. (1994) *Research Methods in Education*. London: Routledge.

Coolican, H. (1994) *Research Methods and Statistics in Psychology*. London: Hodder and Stoughton.

Corr, C. A. (1991) 'Understanding adolescents and death.' In L. S. Shore and D. W. Williams (eds) *Children and Death*. Washington, DC: Hemisphere.

CRUSE (1989) 'Some statistics about death, bereavement and widowhood in Britain' (Leaflet). Newcastle upon Tyne: CRUSE.

Dobson, C. B., Hardy, M., Heyes, S., Humphreys, A. and Humphreys, P. (1981) *Understanding Psychology*. London: Weidenfeld and Nicolson.

Duffy, W. (1995) *Children and Bereavement*. London: National Society, Church House Publishing.

Field, T. and Reite, M. (1984) 'Children's responses to separation from mother during the birth of another child.' *Child Development 55*, 1308–1316.

Fox, S. (1991) 'Psychological tasks of grief.' In L. Goldman (ed) *Life and Loss*. Indiana: Accelerated Development Incorporate.

Freud, S. (1917) 'On mourning and melancholia', reprinted in *On Metapsychiatry, the Theory of Psychoanalysis*. New Orleans: Pelican.

Fried, M. (1962) 'Grieving for a lost home.' In E. J. Dahl (ed) *The Environment of the Metropolis*. New York: Basic Books.

Furman, E. (1974) *A Child's Parent Dies*. New Haven, CT: Yale University Press.

Golding, C. (1991) *Bereavement*. Ramsbury: Crowood.

Goldman, L. (1994) *Life and Loss: A Guide to Helping Grieving Children*. Indiana: Accelerated Learning.

Goldman, L. (1996) *Breaking the Silence: A Guide to Helping Children with Complicated Grief.* Indiana: Accelerated Learning.

Gorer, G. (1965) *Death, Grief and Mourning in Contemporary Britain.* London: Cresset.

Gray, R. (1989) 'Adolescents experiencing the death of a parent.' *Bereavement Care 8*, 2, 17–19.

Grollman, E. A. (1991) 'Explaining death to children and to ourselves.' In L. S. Shore and D. W. Williams (eds) *Children and Death.* Washington, DC: Hemisphere.

Guba, E. G. and Lincoln, Y. S. (1987) 'Naturalistic inquiry.' In M. J. Dunkin (ed) *The International Encyclopaedia of Teaching and Teacher Education.* London: Pergamon.

Heegard, M. (1991) *When Someone Very Special Dies.* Minneapolis, MN: Woodland Press.

Hemmings, P. (1995) 'Social work intervention with bereaved children.' *Journal of Social Work Practice 9*, 2, 109–130.

Hill, O. W. (1969) 'The association of childhood bereavement with suicide attempts in depressive illness.' *British Journal of Psychiatry 115*, 301–304.

Holland, J. M. (1993) 'Child bereavement in Humberside primary schools.' *Educational Research 35*, 3, 289–296.

Holland, J. M. (1997) *Coping with Bereavement: A Handbook for Teachers.* Cardiff: Cardiff Academic Press.

Holland, J. M. (2000) 'Secondary schools and pupil loss by parental bereavement and parental relationship separations.' *Pastoral Care in Education 18*, 4, 33–39.

Holland, J. M. and Ludford, C. (1995) 'The effects of bereavement on children in Humberside secondary schools.' *British Journal of Special Education 22*, 2, 56–59.

Huxley, A. (1977) *The Doors of Perception and Heaven and Hell.* London: Triad Grafton.

Illich, I. (1977) *Limits to Medicine: Medical Nemesis and the Expropriation of Health.* Harmondsworth: Penguin.

Kane, B. (1979) 'Children's concept of death.' *Journal of Genetic Psychology 1*, 134–141.

Kastenbaum, R. (1974) 'Childhood: the kingdom where creatures die.' *Journal of Clinical Child Psychology*, summer, 11–14.

Kelly, A. (1955) *The Psychology of Personal Constructs.* New York: Norton.

Kingston upon Hull City Council, Learning Services (2000) *Lost for Words. Loss Education Training Package*, City Psychological Service, Essex House, Kingston upon Hull.

Knapman, K. (1993) 'Supporting the bereaved child at school.' In P. Alsop and P. McCaffery (eds) *How to Cope with Childhood Loss.* London: Longman.

Kranzler, E., Schaefer, D., Wasserman, G. and Davies, M. (1990) 'Early childhood bereavement.' *Journal of the American Academy of Child and Adolescent Psychiatry 29*, 4, 513–520.

Kubler-Ross, E. (1982) *On Death and Dying.* London: Tavistock.

Kubler-Ross, E. (1983) *On Children and Death.* New York: Macmillan.

Kubler-Ross, E. (1991) *Life after Death.* Berkeley, CA: Celestial Arts.

Lamers, W. D. (1986) 'Helping the child to grieve.' In G. H. Patterson (ed) *Children and Death.* London, Ont.: Kings College.

Leaman, O. (1995) *Death and Loss: Compassionate Approaches in the Classroom.* London: Cassell.

Leckley, J. (1991) 'Attitudes and responses to death education of a sample of primary school teachers in Belfast.' *Bereavement Care 10*, 2, 22–23.

Lee, R. M. (1993) *Doing Research on Sensitive Topics.* London: Sage.

LeShan, E. (1979) *Learning to Say Goodbye: When a Parent Dies.* New York: Macmillan.

Lewis, J. (1992) 'Death and divorce – helping students cope in single parent families.' *NASSP Bulletin 76*, 543, 55–60.

Loftus, E. F. (1975) 'Leading questions and the eye witness report.' *Cognitive Psychology 7*, 560–572.

Lovell, K. (1973) *Educational Psychology and Children.* Sevenoaks: Hodder and Stoughton.

Ludford, C. (1994) 'Children, death and bereavement.' Unpublished MEd dissertation, University of Hull.

Marris, P. (1958) *Widows and their Families.* London: Routledge and Kegan Paul.

Marshall, F. (1993) *Losing a Parent.* London: Sheldon.

Martin, A. (1983) 'An annotated bibliography of literature dealing with the need for death education.' *Education 229*, 360.

Mishne, J. (1992) 'The grieving child: manifest and hidden losses in childhood and adolescence.' *Child and Adolescent Social Work 9*, 6, 471–490.

Moser, C. A. and Kalton, G. (1977) *Survey Methods in Social Investigation.* London: Heinemann Educational.

Musty, E. (1990) 'Children, death and grief.' *Religious Education Today 7*, 2, 14–15.

Neisser, U. (1982) *Memory Observed.* London: W. H. Freeman.

Office for National Statistics (1997) *Mortality Statistics.* Fareham: Crown.

Office for National Statistics (1999) *Health Statistics Quarterly 4* (1991–98). Fareham: Crown.

Parkes, C. M. (1986) *Studies of Grief in Adult Life.* Madison, WI: International Press.

Pattison, E. M. (1976) 'The fatal myth of death in the family.' *American Journal of Psychiatry 133*, 6, 50–54.

Piaget, J. (1929) *The Child's Concept of the World.* London: Routledge and Kegan Paul.

Pickard, W. (1999) 'Be prepared for the unthinkable.' *Times Educational Supplement*, 30 April, 3.

Raphael, B. (1982) 'The young child and the death of a parent.' In C. M. Parkes and L. Stevenson-Hinde (eds) *The Place of Attachment in Human Behaviour.* London: Tavistock.

Raphael, B. (1984) *Anatomy of Bereavement: A Handbook for the Caring Professions.* London: Hutchinson.

Rinpoché, S. (1992) *The Tibetan Book of Living and Dying.* San Francisco: HarperCollins.

Rochlin, G. (1967) 'How younger children view death and themselves.' In G. Grollman (ed) *Explaining Death to Children.* Boston, MA: Beacon.

Rosenblatt, R. C. (1988) 'Grief: the social context of private feelings.' *Journal of Social Issues 44*, 3, 67–78.

Rowling, L. (1994) 'Loss and grief in the context of a health promoting school.' Unpublished PhD thesis, University of Southampton.

Rowling, L. (1995) 'The disenfranchized grief of teachers.' *Journal of Death and Dying 31*, 4, 321–323.

Rowling, L. and Holland, J. M. (2000) 'A comparative study of grief and suicide in English and Australian Schools.' *Death Studies 24*, 35–50.

Rubin, D. C. and Kozin, M. (1984) 'Vivid memories.' *Cognition 16*, 81–85.

Rutter, M. (1966) *Children of Sick Parents.* London: Oxford University Press.

Sanders, C. (1995) 'Grief of children and parents.' In K. Dorka (ed) *Children Mourning, Mourning Children.* Washington, DC: Hospice Foundation of America.

Schaefer, D. and Lyons, C. (1986) *How Do We Tell the Children?* New York: Newmarket Press.

Sharp, S. and Cowie, H. (1998) *Counselling and Supporting Children in Distress.* London: Sage Publications.

Shoor, M. and Speed, M. (1963) 'Death, delinquency and the mourning process.' In R. Fulton (ed) *Death and Identity.* Bowie, MD: Charles Press.

Silverman, P. R. and Klass, D. (1996) 'What's the problem?' In D. Klass, P. R. Silverman and S. L. Nickman *Continuing Bonds.* Washington, DC: Taylor and Francis.

Sisterton, D. (1983) 'Counselling in the primary school.' *Division of Educational Child Psychology, Educational Section Review 7,* 2, 10–15.

Taylor, L. (1983) *Mourning Dress: A Costume and Social History.* London: Allen and Unwin.

Tschudin, V. and Marks-Maran, D. (1992) *Ethics.* London: Baillière Tindall.

Tulving, E. (1972) 'Episodic and semantic memory.' In E. Tulving and W. Donaldson (eds) *Organisation of Memory.* New York: Academic Press.

Turner, V. (1969) *The Ritual Process.* Chicago: Aldine.

Urbanowicz, M. (1994) 'Teaching about grief and loss: a whole school approach.' *Bereavement Care 3,* 1, 8.

Van der Veer, R. and Valsiner, J. (1994) *The Vygotskian Reader.* Oxford: Blackwell.

Walker, R. (1989) *Doing Research: A Handbook for Teachers.* London: Routledge.

Ward, B. (1993) *Good Grief 2: Exploring Feelings, Loss and Death with Over-11s.* London: Jessica Kingsley Publishers.

Ward, B. (1994) *Healing Grief.* London: Vermilion.

Wass, H. and Corr, C. A. (1984) *Childhood and Death.* New York: Hemisphere.

Weller, E. B., Weller, R. A., Fristad, M. A., Cain, S. E. and Bowes, J. M. (1988) 'Should children attend their parent's funeral?' *Journal of the American Academy of Child and Adolescent Psychiatry 27,* 559–562.

Wolff, S. (1992) *Children under Stress.* Harmondsworth: Penguin.

Worden, W. (1984) *Grief Counselling and Grief Therapy.* London: Tavistock.

World Medical Assembly (1964) *Declaration of Helsinki,* 18th World Medical Assembly, Helsinki, Finland.

Wright, B. (1989) 'Sudden death: nurses' reactions and relatives' opinions.' *Bereavement Care 8,* 1, 1.

Yamamoto, J. (1970) 'Cultural factors in loneliness, death, and separation.' *Medical Times 98*, 177–183.

Yule, W. and Gold, A. (1993) *Wise before the Event.* London: Calouste.

Zach, H. (1978) 'Children and death.' *Social Work Today 9*, 39, 11–13.

Music

Abba (1981) 'The way friends do', in *Super Trouper*, Polydor Records, London.

Blondie (1979) 'Die young, stay pretty', in *Eat to the Beat*, Chrysalis Records, Los Angeles.

Bob Dylan (1963) 'A hard rain's gonna fall', in *The Freewheelin'*, Electra/Asylum/Nonesuch Records, New York.

Led Zeppelin (1971) 'Stairway to heaven', in *Led Zeppelin*, Atlantic Records, New York.

Mike and the Mechanics (1988) 'The living years', in *The Living Years*, Atlantic Records, New York.

Index

Abrams, R. 44, 98
abstract thought 166
abuse 177, 195
  see also particular types of abuse
academic work see school work
acceptance of loss 30, 72, 87, 146,
  190–1
acknowledgement of loss 30, 195
  in school 106, 109, 111, 191
acquired immune deficiency
  syndrome (AIDS) 51
adolescents 51
  death of sibling 47
  post bereavement effects 39, 48
  and school 42, 120–1
adults
  approachability 14, 190, 191
  and parental death 23
  role in bereavement 9
  support from 24, 187, 194
age
  and loss type 174–5
  and perception of school 103
  and post bereavement effects 40,
    96–7, 119, 161
  and recall of events 127
  and role models 162
  and understanding of death
    77–8, 166–72
aggression 16, 38
alcohol use/abuse 136
Alder, J. 48
anger/anger-type reactions 184
  after death 128, 130, 146, 148,
    165
    six months 132, 136
    one year 141
    two years 144, 145
  at bad news 29, 71
  in bereavement 16–17, 37, 38,
    195

at exclusion from rituals 84, 88,
  89
anniversaries 138–9, 141, 143
antisocial behaviour 39, 140
Archer, J. 21
Ariès, P. 21
attachment 20, 50, 172
  loss 14, 173–4, 175–6, 179
  and recall of death 73
avoidance 153
  of bereaved 24, 123
  of reality by bereaved 37
  of topic of death 47, 109

Balk, D. 47
Bannister, P. et al. 54
Barnsley, N. 25, 31
Barraclough, B. see Bunch, J. et al.
Bartlett, F.C. 57
Beck Depression Inventory 40
behaviour difficulties 194, 195
  in bereavement 16, 37, 38, 101
bereavement 12, 19, 21–2, 30
  childhood 36–41
    longer-term effects 39–40,
      151–65, 183, 193
    short-term effects 37–8
  preparation 43, 44, 104
  training gap 15
  transition period 25
bereavement loss 14, 173, 178,
  179
  outcome 175–6
bias, interviewer 55
Birtchell, T. (1970) 40
Birtchell, T. (1975) 39
Blackburn, M. 51
body, viewing 21, 25, 26
  see also chapel of rest
bonding 73
Bowes, J.M. see Weller, E.B. et al.
Bowlby, J. (1963) 39
Bowlby, J. (1973) 50
Branwhite, T. 36
Brown, G.W. et al. 155